LOG CABINS
AND HOW TO BUILD THEM

LOG CABINS
AND HOW TO BUILD THEM

WILLIAM SWANSON

THE LYONS PRESS
GUILFORD, CONNECTICUT
AN IMPRINT OF THE GLOBE PEQUOT PRESS

Library of Congress Cataloging-in-Publication Data
is available on file.

ISBN 1-58574-254-6

Manufactured in the United States of America
First Lyons Press edition/Third printing

*This book is dedicated to
my grandparents
who settled in the wild timber section
of Minnesota
shortly after the Civil War.
They built a log cabin,
where my mother lived from infancy
to young womanhood.*

FOREWORD

The author has traveled the length and breadth of our land from Texas to Minnesota, from the Pacific coast to the Atlantic, always building with a thought of bettering his fellow man's home. In this book the step-by-step text and illustrations will give an inexperienced builder a true picture of how a log cabin can be built by various time- and labor-saving methods. A cabin creation planned and built by one's own hands is appreciated far more and brings a feeling of satisfaction and pride never felt by one who has simply bought his cabin. The types of construction presented in this book are all practical and given with the view of imparting to the inexperienced builder the best and easiest method of building a log cabin.

The author is deeply indebted to the following for their cooperation and assistance: Ringwood Company of Erskine Lakes, N. J.; Pinecliff Lake Realty Company of New Jersey; The State Development Commissions of Maine, Pennsylvania, and New York; Virginia Conservation Commission; Oregon State Highway Commission. For data on fireplaces and their equipment I am indebted to the Bennet Fireplace Company of Norwich, New York, and the Donley Brothers Company of Cleveland, Ohio.

WILLIAM E. SWANSON

CONTENTS

Chapter 1

BUILDING PROCEDURE

After the foundation has been placed, the cabin wall can be built, leaving the overhanging ends to be cut off later. The logs should be lifted up into place with the help of a jim pole, or pulled up on sliding logs, using a block and tackle on each end. This will eliminate a large amount of heavy work. The logs should be fitted into place on the wall. A good mechanic can fit a log on the ground and then put it in place. Make certain that the butt ends of the log fit properly against window and door jambs which are usually 2-inch or 3-inch planking. If a butt cut does not fit properly, hold the log in its proper place and run the timber saw between the butt and the jamb until it fits.

All logs should be flattened slightly on each other's laying surface or trimmed slightly with the axe if they are round. Drift pins or dowels should be placed in the wall to keep the wall in line or to prevent a log from sliding off another log between a corner and a door jamb. Supports, for holding a log while working on it, can be placed on uprights forming a scaffold. Or, if logs are long enough to extend beyond the corner wall, planks may be placed on these extensions and used as a platform for working on a log or chinking or oiling. When the work is finished the surplus ends can be cut as desired. The various types of wall corners will be described in another section of this book.

The roofing of a log cabin is important. To frame the roof of heavy peeled timber gives a pioneer effect, but cutting roof boards from slabs is a slow, tedious and expensive process unless done at a mill.

Making shingles by hand is a difficult procedure to one who is inexperienced or unskilled, and the final result may be a leaky roof. Homemade shingles, which are usually 20 to 26 inches long, in order to give a pioneer effect, are laid over a heavy roofing paper that has been placed on $7/8$-inch roofing boards. If 16-inch cedar shingles are used, the rows should be laid to the weather not more than 5 inches apart with the joints at least 1 inch away from the under-joint. There are many good types of roofing, such as asphalt or asbestos shingles, that can be used. Much depends on the amount of money that the owner is willing to spend.

The fireplace should rest solidly on the stone foundation and should be made of stone or brick with a flue lining inside. If the fireplace is to be placed in the end wall, half outside and half inside, the chimney should be massive enough to hold the butt end of the wall logs in place. The wall can be built up without the fireplace, which can be built in after; in this case brace the ends of the logs in such a way that they do not interfere with the building of the chimney and fireplace. Take special care to flash the roof and the chimney so that there will be no leaks.

Floors are important for many reasons. They must stand a great deal of abuse from wet feet, heavy footwear, and the change of weather conditions.

If a log beam floor is to be laid and a heavy plank floor placed over the beams, the floor must be fitted around the hearth of the fireplace, not under it. This type of floor is satisfactory provided the basement is accessible for storage of garden tools, etc., but should it be inaccessible it would harbor mice, etc. If it is at all possible, fill the cabin to the floor level with tamped earth and then put a 3-inch concrete floor on it. It can later be covered with a $1/8$-inch mastic tile which is cheap, neat in appearance, easy to take care of, and fire-resisting. A stone flagging floor, filled in between with $1/2$-inch mortar joints, makes a neat floor at very little cost provided flat stones can be found on the property. However, they are apt to scale by continuous use and frequent washing. Seven-eighths-inch fir flooring, painted on the under side and placed over 2 x 10 inch joists on 16-inch centers, and covered with a cheap grade of linoleum makes a neat and economical floor.

WALL PROCEDURE

The first wall logs are placed flat on the foundation. In the case of a long wall it may be more advisable to splice the logs rather than place a log that is too small on one end in the wall. Place the long side wall logs in first and then proceed with the center beam which supports the floor joist at a level that is approximately 8 inches below the top of the expected floor joist height. The supporting member of the center beam is made of short logs which rest on large flat stones, or, if no stones are to be had, make a footing of cement and sand. The floor joists can be fastened into the side logs with a tenon and be well spiked. After the joists are all in place, the floor of planks should be installed. If the floor is to be made of dressed 2 x 10 inch planking with 16 inches joist center to center, floored over with a 1-inch flooring, the joist should be cut into the side beams for anchor. *(Fig. 1.)*

The chimney with its fireplace can be built on the outside of the wall or in the wall, depending on the builder's wishes.

The wall procedure is a matter which is up to the individual and depends on whether the window and door openings are to be cut out but not framed in until the walls are finished. The walls can be chinked with oakum but finished later, as there is no set rule about when chinking is done, but it is preferable to finish after the logs have settled a little and dried out. Many log cabins have been built by men with no special ability, but who still make a fairly neat job of it.

If the logs are short and splicing must be resorted to, the builder should see to it that the joints are approximately the same diameter and that the splicings are not too close to each other. If short lengths between windows or doors are walled up and no window or door jamb is used, a temporary brace must be placed against it to prevent it from moving away from the alignment. Where a window and door are placed close together—that is, less than 1 foot—it will be foolhardy to place short horizontal lengths of logs as mullion walls between them because the drilling and driving of drift pins

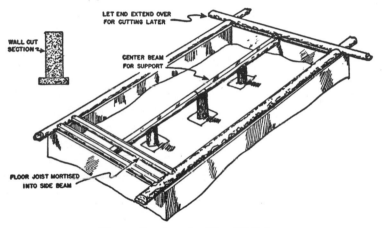

Fig. 1   Starting the First Wall Log

will split these short logs and a repair job will soon become necessary. Although the short length may show no sign of splitting when the cabin is built, it may be checked by the weather later and fall apart. It is best to use vertical logs as mullion, which is the name applied to a support separating two windows.

Do not attempt to cut the ends of the logs used in building up the walls until later, and if they extend over the end walls for a distance of 3 to 5 feet, let them remain unless there is need for short lengths and you are short of timbers. When the wall is finished the ends should be cut off using wood strips nailed on each side to guide the double hand saw, or following a vertical plumb line or a raked line as desired.

There are many types of corners as shown in this book, but if this is your first attempt at building a log cabin and you have had no previous building experience of any kind, do not attempt a difficult type such as the cupped corner. That one really takes a good mechanic. Pick out the simple type of corner for your first attempt, and if the results are good, a more difficult type of corner can be used on the next cabin. If you have the guidance of professional help, you can try a difficult type of corner without fear of failure, but in this case the cost of the cabin may be more than anticipated.

Do not make the mistake of building a cabin which is beyond your financial means, as it may never be finished. Insure your cabin against theft if it is in an isolated spot and against loss from fire as there is danger from brush fires. Lock and board up the home when leaving it for the winter if it is to be unoccupied.

STARTING THE WALL

The walls are started with the larger timbers on the bottom to avoid much back-breaking labor. In this particular case the logs are full and have not been trimmed for the top and bottom surfaces, but have been cleaned with an axe and draw knife.

The first floor is laid on timber stringers which rest on the cross beams. These in turn are placed on the longitudinal beams that rest on the foundation piers.

The fireplace and chimney can be built before the side walls are set up. This method of construction is optional. In many cases the walls are set up first and the chimney built around it. The copper roof flashing is imbedded into the chimney, which is made of field stones, and flat stones are used for the fireplace mantel. The flue lining is 13 inches by 13 inches, outside measurements, or approximately 12 inches by 12 inches inside measurements. In order to have a good draft, the area of the fireplace opening should not be more than 10 square feet. If it is made larger the smoke will not leave by way of the chimney and may fill the room on a calm day.

As the walls progress to the height of the eaves the scaffold can be built up making it strong enough to carry the weight necessary in handling the timber. While building, the walls are kept on an even height around the entire structure. A small inside chimney is built at one end for the use of a stove in the kitchen. The ridge timber and the longitudinal purlin timbers should be exceptionally straight, prize specimens of timbers which make for a straighter roof.

The rafters are smaller roof timbers that are about 6 to 8 inches in diameter on the larger end, and smaller at the top end.

If a porch is to be added the porch roof longitudinal timber is 10 inches in diameter. This timber rests on the three vertical posts which must be strong enough to carry not only the porch roof but the heavy snowfall common to the northern regions.

Chapter 2

TYPES OF CABINS

WHAT TYPE OF CABIN WILL BE MOST SUITABLE?

Cabins of slab logs nailed to vertical studs or stood on end against horizontal plates have been built. In some cases slabs merely placed on a frame sheathed house have served the purpose. This style of camouflage can hardly be considered a log cabin even though the special milled 8-inch log cabin siding so popular for pioneer tavern fronts is used. It is merely a frame house with a false dressing.

Logs milled to a thickness of 10 inches or 8 inches, leaving regular chamfered edges so that chinking can be placed into small joints makes a neat job, but the extra cost of milling will offset the time for construction.

Where timber is scarce and stone plentiful there are two styles of log cabins that can be built. One is the half stone and half log cabin, which has a stone wall up to the window sill all around the house, or it may be better to build a stone house and use timbers for the roof and floors.

The pictures which follow offer suggestions for types of cabins that are suitable for locations along lakes, hillsides, etc., and can, of course, be adapted to other types of setting.

WEEK-END LOG HUT

Many dream of a place to enjoy a quiet week end in the woods where meals can be cooked and a few bunks can be used for sleeping purposes.

7

This hut has an upper floor that can be used for sleeping or storage. *(Fig. 2.)* The porch is roomy with its high roof providing space where canoes or boats can be stored. A long broad seat is placed on one side of the porch. The porch floor can be made of 6-inch concrete slabs or flagging. The floor of the hut is made of concrete with a covering of ⅛-inch mastic tile. On the first floor there is one door and one window in the front, and one window on each side. The

Fig. 2   Week-End Log Hut

upper floor has four windows, one in the rear, one in the front, and one in each dormer on the sides of the roof.

There is no room for a fireplace in this hut but space can be allotted for the cook stove in one corner. The walls of the cooking space should be covered with wire lath and plastered with concrete containing lime to make a fire-resisting wall. The chimney is made of concrete blocks or cobblestones and has an 8-inch by 8-inch flue lining.

All windows can be double hung, or made so that they

can be held in place by window spring bolts, which are locked into holes in the window jamb. Since this is a week-end hut it is preferable to have the windows provided with shutters that can be easily removed and tucked away, or hinged on the outside or inside. The one main room should be 16 feet by 24 feet, with an additional 10 feet for the porch added to the length.

LAKE SHORE LOG CABIN

The foundation for this type of lake shore cottage is made of field stone. *(Figs. 3 and 4.)* This kind of location will be a bleak spot on a cold windy day. Trees should be planted at about a radius of 200 feet from the house as a protection from the wind.

The floor plan shows how it can be utilized for two families with one bedroom for each. The outside entrance can be floored with flagging or discarded 1-inch marble slabs broken up into random pieces. When laying, keep the floor smooth and have it slope toward the outer step with a pitch of 3 inches per 12 feet to make it drain readily. A basement boat-storage room and work shop can be built to round out the hominess of this cabin.

LCG CABIN ON STILTS

A cabin built on stilts in a swampy region is a trapper's dream. *(Fig. 5.)* Here one need not be afraid that some animal will steal or eat things left on the elevated porch. The occupant will be able to see over the tall grass or shrubbery at all times, and the space under the cabin will provide shelter for a boat or automobile. The four corners of the cabin are supported by 16-inch-diameter posts imbedded 4 feet into the ground upon large flat stones. These posts should first be soaked in a half-and-half mixture of creosote and kerosene for twenty-four hours. The logs have notched corners and

Fig. 3 Lake Shore Log Cabin

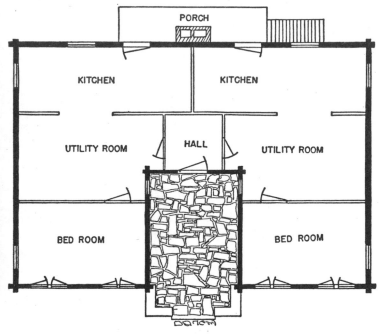

Fig. 4 Floor Plan

the floor beams are notched into the cross beams which extend beyond the wall to act also as a support for the porch. The cross beams rest directly on the corner posts. The roof is made of 2-inch by 4-inch rafters with shiplap roofing boards covered with sheet roofing paper to shed the water.

Fig. 5   Log Cabin on Stilts

HALF LOG CABIN

In locations where it is desirable to build a log cabin, the timber may not be the correct thickness or quality, and only a limited number of logs can be secured from the surrounding land. The cabin, in this case, would be more or less an imported proposition. The cost of trucking and paying for the additional logs make a full log cabin expensive. To remedy this, a half log cabin can be built with free stone as a substitute, and yet the cabin will give all the pioneer effect that is desired. Free stones along a river or creek bed, and a little ability at bonding is all that is needed to build the walls and key the logs into the stone wall. The stone joints should be lapped within a reasonable distance, keeping the corners plumb. An inexperienced individual may surprise himself at his ability as a mason.

Figure 6 shows a cabin built where there is an abundance of free stone, and walls of stone are built up to the window sill. From this level, logs are used to carry the wall up to the

Fig. 6   Half Log Cabin

first floor plate line. The balance of the building is of frame work construction. Flooring consists of mastic tile over a concrete slab. The logs in this case have been sized to an 8-inch dimension with a slab cut from all four sides, leaving four flat surfaces with rounded edges between each, and chinked with small joints.

TYPE OF CONSTRUCTION

Another type of half-log cabin has its side walls built of logs and its end walls of stone. *(Fig. 7)* A fireplace is built into the center of the stone-end wall. The butt ends of the side-wall logs are embedded into the stone-end walls which extend approximately 1 foot beyond the side walls. The roof in this type of a cabin is a heavy beamed one, but the end wall must extend at least a foot above the roof line for efficient flashing against the roof.

Fig. 7   Half Stone and Log Cabin

Fig. 8   Stone Cottage

STONE COTTAGE

A stone cabin can be built wherever trees for a log cabin are scarce. *(Fig. 8.)* This drawing shows a 4-wall construction with a roof sloping toward the front and a small ranch type front porch. The walls could be built of quarry or loose cobble-stone. A wooden lintel over each window, a plank door, and French windows are suggested. The foundation should have a reinforced footing 12 inches high by 22 inches wide, and the walls can be 12 to 14 inches thick. If the building is to

Fig. 9   Skiing Hut Built for Heavy Snow Load on the Roof

have a finished coat of cement on the outside and inside, do not fill up the mortar joints as the rough plaster coat needs the dug-out joints as a means of binding to the wall.

SKI HUT

This hut is built with walls that slope inward toward the top and are called raked walls. *(Fig.9.)* The roof is made of the same strong logs as are used in building the side walls, so as to give a very substantial roof for heavy snow loads. The roofing boards or slabs are nailed over these roof logs and then covered with a suitable roofing material. This cabin

Fig. 10   A Comfy Log Cabin

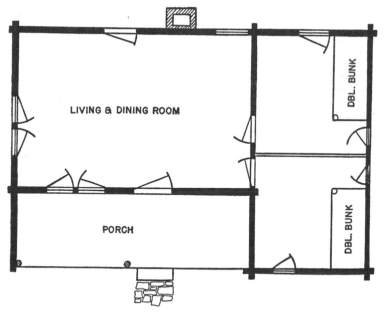

LIVING & DINING ROOM

DBL. BUNK

DBL. BUNK

PORCH

Fig. 11   Floor Plan

should be built long and narrow with a steep roof to allow the snow to slide off the roof easily. In ski territory where plenty of snow is needed there may be more snowfall than the usual roof will carry and a person would feel secure to know that, regardless of how much had fallen on his ski hut, the roof would not give way.

COMFY LOG CABIN

This three-room cabin is easy to build. *(Figs. 10 and 11.)* By extending one end wall and the roof a protected porch is added. Flagging, embedded in concrete, forms the floor of the porch. The entire side walls are made of 8-inch to 10-inch logs resting on a stone footing. The windows are casement style and are swung inward so that screens can be put on the outside. A small fireplace or a chimney for cooking is placed at the back of the living room which also serves as the dining room. A floor plan shows double bunks for sleeping purposes, with two windows in each room.

RUSSIAN TYPE LOG CABIN

This type of log cabin is an early Russian or Finnish style with grass or mud roof. *(Fig. 12.)* The roof is more or less a constant repair job if made of mud, which is hardly sanitary unless a tar felt is laid underneath, but the earth fill has the one advantage that it keeps the house cool in hot weather. Some Laplanders plant grass and vegetation on the sod roof to keep the soil in place. The roof beams must be made very heavy to support the heavy load of earth that forms the roofing surface. A grass roof will need approximately the degree of slope shown, but for a mud roof, the slope should not be over 1 foot per 12 feet of length.

MOUNTAIN HOME

Many owners prefer to have a two story cabin home. *(Fig. 13.)* This type of cabin may be built in the rocky hills or

Fig. 12   Russian Type Log Cabin

Fig. 13   Mountain Home

glen where a small flat area is available and stones are plentiful. A nearby supply of timber is also desirable. This home has no full basement but could have a little round cellar under the ground floor. The first floor walls are built of fieldstone to a height of 10 feet, with a door in front and windows on each side wall. The overhang of the first floor is to be made by the extension of the floor beams of the second floor, and with a slight sloping pitch of 3 inches in 3 feet. By having such an overhang there is no possibility of hailstones breaking the first floor windows.

The second story floor is formed of 1½-inch tongue and groove flooring on beams, which are set on 2 foot centers. The logs are then placed in the wall to the level of the second story eaves, and the rafters set on the roof from this point. The ends of the dormers are spaced up with studs, boarded up with shiplap, and then covered with beveled siding made from logs. The windows of the second floor are placed one on each side of the chimney, and a double window on the other end. The chimney is built in the wall of the first floor and carried up to a distance of 2 feet above the roof. The flue lining is double to take care of a fireplace on the first floor, and also a stove on the second floor.

SQUARED TIMBER CABIN

Cabins that are made with timber that has been squared or has a slight cambered edge on the outside are easy to build. *(Figs. 14 and 15.)* The cutting of the logs is merely a matter of squaring and fitting them together, using any one of the various types of corners that one may choose. To build this type of wall it is best to dowel the logs together with 1-inch hardwood dowels or trunnels made of maple, hickory, or birch. This will be a great deal cheaper than iron rods.

The window frames should be made of 2-inch material

Fig. 14   Squared Timber Cabin

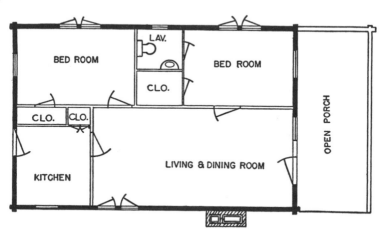

Fig. 15   Floor Plan

rabbeted on the inside for French windows, and rabbeted on the outside for screen windows.

The foundation and fireplace are tied together and the side walls keyed into the chimney wall. A large saddle is placed on the roof side to throw the water away from the chimney.

A large front porch runs the whole width of the house, with a rail built up of logs.

DOUBLE FAMILY LOG CABIN

This cabin is large enough to house two families, with two fireplaces built either in the center of the building as shown, or at the ends. *(Figs. 16 and 17.)* The center of the building is left open with the roof over it and acts as a corridor or porch for each apartment. The building covers a very large space on the ground and needs a stone foundation, whether built with a full basement or not. The corner ends are cut on a slanting vertical line of 1 foot every 6 feet off the plumb line. The windows on all bedrooms are 4 feet off the floor line but the other windows can be 26 inches off the floor level. All screens are placed on the outside with an outside covering of ½-inch wire screen to prevent raccoons or other prowling animals from jumping on the window sill or tearing the screens at night. A plan view is shown with three bedrooms to each apartment, and without a lavatory.

MILLED SURFACE LOG CABIN

A cabin built partly of stone and partly of mill-dressed timber is shown here. *(Fig. 18.)* The basement is full size, made of quarry stone and built 8 feet deep. The overhang of the roof is braced by forming the corners so that they project beyond the wall line. If the distance is over 12 feet, a bracket should be placed in between to keep the eave-lines straight.

Fig. 16 Two Family Log Cabin

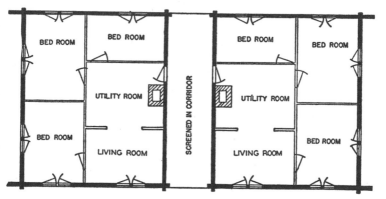

Fig. 17 Floor Plan

An open porch with a timber rail around three sides should be built on a stone foundation that is filled with dirt. A 4-inch thick concrete slab on top of the dirt fill should meet the front door sill. The concrete porch floor should slope toward the two outlet holes for rain water drainage. The slope of the concrete slab should be 1½ inches to 2 inches in 6 feet. The timber should be well creosoted and filled with

Fig. 18   Milled Surface Timber Cabin

chinking to prevent heavy checking. To beautify the wood surface a novel finish can be made on the outside weather surface by gouging short troughs in the surface with a 1-inch round edge gouge chisel or a scrub plane.

LOG CABIN BESIDE A STONY CREEK

This particular cabin *(figs. 19 and 20)* has the kitchen and the adjacent bedroom sunken below the level of the other rooms. There are two smaller bedrooms, while the dining room and parlor are combined into one room 12 feet wide by 20 feet long. The fireplace is placed at one end of the living-dining room. The entrance door between the living room and the porch has glass panes to help brighten the living room. All rooms have one or more windows and the two doors that

Fig. 19   Log Cabin Beside a Stony Creek

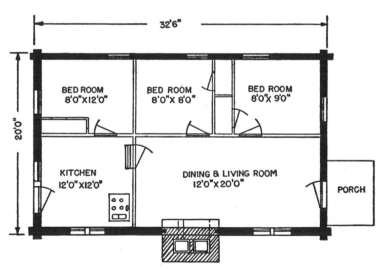

Fig. 20   Floor Plan

lead from the two bedrooms into the living room have frosted glass in them to admit as much light as possible to the living room.

CABIN ON A HIGH RIDGE

This illustration shows a cabin placed on a hilltop overlooking a valley, with the porch and part of the house on stilts. *(Figs. 21 and 22.)* The walls are square hewn logs with dovetailed corners. A fireplace is shown in the living room. The attic dormer of the house has a vertical slab covering the bottom end, being cut diamond shape. The roof can be covered with shingles or other surface. If the footing for the house is placed on stones, make certain the posts are properly imbedded in the side of the hill. This also applies to that part of the house that rests over the ridge. The chimney can be made of cobblestones placed around the flue lining and plastered with white Portland cement to make the chimney surface smooth. The logs should be calked with oakum and then filled with white calking compound to give beauty and satisfactory waterproofing results.

CABIN BY A LAKE

Who does not long for a cabin overlooking a lake where one can fish. This cabin *(fig. 23)* has a full basement which should be above the high water line to keep it dry. If the ground is sandy or of soft soil, the footing must be very large to avoid any settling in ground moistened by water of the lake. If building on a stony shore where the stones are in solid formation, there need be no fear of settling of the foundation. The foundation, 18 inches thick, should be laid into the rock.

Four windows and a door on the lake side provide light, ventilation, and view over the lake. The first floor entrance

Fig. 21   Cabin on a High Ridge

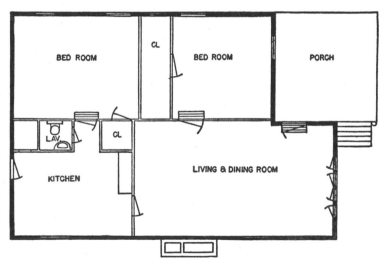

Fig. 22   Floor Plan

from the roadway does not appear in the drawing of the cabin but is seen in the plan. *(Fig. 24.)* All windows are French type, swinging inward. There are four rooms with a fireplace in the living room. A porch is built out over the lake to a distance of 8 feet or more, as desired. The roof is covered with any type of shingles, fireproof preferred. The chimney

Fig. 23   Cabin by a Lake

has two flue linings, one for the fireplace and one for the cook stove, which may be either on the first floor or the basement. For sewage disposal a watertight cesspool is recommended, but the roof drains should not lead into the cesspool. Trees around the cabin would make it cooler in hot weather, but tree limbs should not touch the cabin for fear of scratching the painted surface.

The basement plan *(fig. 25)* shows a dining room with a view over the lake, a storage room for wood or other fuel, and a room for a small workshop. The boiler room is in the

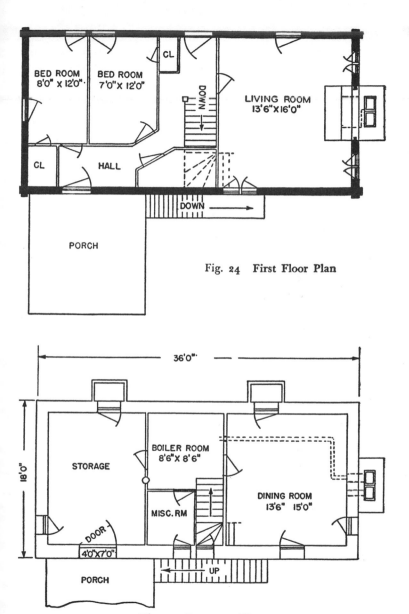

Fig. 24   First Floor Plan

BED ROOM
8'0" x 12'0"

BED ROOM
7'0" x 12'0"

CL

DOWN

LIVING ROOM
13'6" X 16'0"

CL

HALL

DOWN →

PORCH

36'0"

18'0"

STORAGE

BOILER ROOM
8'6" X 8'6"

MISC. RM

DINING ROOM
13'6" 15'0"

DOOR

4'0" X 7'0"

PORCH

UP

Fig. 25   Basement Plan

center. An inside stairway leads from the dining room to the first floor. The main floor has a living room and two bedrooms, each having a closet. An outside porch overlooking the lake and extending over the shore line, with the posts placed into the water, makes an interesting as well as useful layout, but the posts must be well anchored. A stairway leads from the porch down to the lake shore to make an easy entrance to the basement for storage of boats or for bathing purposes.

Chapter 3

SELECTING A LOCATION

In seeking a good location for a camp a number of factors should be taken into consideration to insure health, safety and maximum enjoyment. A pure water supply is essential. Firewood or other fuel must be available; sunny exposure for cool days, and shade with a breeze from prevailing winds for warm days are desirable, of course.

Suitable timber on or adjacent to the site for log construction and near-by beds of stone for a fireplace will save on construction costs. If the cabin is to be built on a lake, the logs can be floated in. A good location along a lake is at a point with a rise that forms part of a sheltering cove for boats. A sandy bathing beach within walking distance of camp is desirable.

Much of the enjoyment of camping out comes from just watching the ever-changing distant scene. A porch from which can be viewed nature's colorful sunset masterpieces, the mists of evening settling down over distant hills, or the far end of a lake, adds much to the overall quiet enjoyment. If sunrise can also be seen from the site there will be even greater enjoyment for fishermen and other early risers.

The music of a mountain stream and the rustle of the wind through the tops of evergreens are events that nature lovers will travel miles to enjoy. A location beside a dashing brook is a constant joy, and on the practical side, it will probably be fed by a near-by spring which will solve the water problem, making possible a spring house in which butter, cream, meats and water can be kept cold and fresh in summer.

A log cabin should not be too close to a well traveled highway unless the owner wishes to entertain visitors who "just happened to be passing by" about meal time. On the other hand it should not be so deep in the woods that moving air and sunlight are shut out. One of the worst mistakes is to build on a low spot that may be subject to spring overflow or that is close to a mosquito-breeding swamp.

If it is to be a summer vacation home and you have a car, distance is not so important a consideration. You won't want to spend more than three or four hours traveling each way. If you want to give consideration to office friends and acquaintances you can figure that most of them out on a Sunday drive will not travel beyond a 50-mile radius.

COST OF CONSTRUCTION

Cost of construction is an important consideration with respect to location. If you have to build a road to a site on the side of a mountain, and haul men and materials from a distant city to build the cabin, costs will mount rapidly. The farther you are away from civilization the more the transportation costs increase. If you and a friend intend to do most of the work yourselves and utilize building materials on the site you may disregard this factor. If it is to be a family camp and the desires of the family are consulted the decision finally made will be to limit the distance to within a day's drive of home.

If you intend to do part of the work yourself and the cabin is to be a modest sized structure, an experienced log cabin builder—not necessarily a carpenter—will be a big help. He will know what kind of timber in the locality it is best to use, how to cut and cure the logs, and how to build the structure. He will probably be able to furnish a helper. With proper equipment, and perhaps the special assistance of a stone mason to build the chimney and lay a concrete foundation, a small log cabin can be built in two or three weeks.

HIRING AN ARCHITECT

For more ornate structures it is best to consult an architect who has designed and built modern log cabins. This will insure sound construction and artistic interior finish and fixtures that will do much to make the summer home comfortable. The furniture of a log cabin should not be cast-offs from some garret or furniture warehouse, but should be made on the site and in rustic style. The architect can furnish sketches which will permit the future owner to see just what he is getting and to check off anything in the plans and specifications he does not think will be worth the expense. The architect will locate a good local contractor and building-material supply dealer and arrange for bringing necessary materials to the site when needed. The architect can design the type of structure that best fits the family needs. His fee will add from 5 to 8 per cent to the overall cost, but his experienced judgment and supervision of the job will avoid costly mistakes and insure low future upkeep.

GETTING THE SITE

There are many ways to obtain a site for the cabin after you have worked out general details and allowable costs and decided on the district you wish to locate in. Some of these can be briefly enumerated:

1. Find out from neighbors, or from county officials, the name and residence of the party who owns the land. Contact the owner and ask him to quote a price for the size plot you want to purchase. If you want to rent the site, he can have an agreement drawn up for a 5-, 10-, or 15-year period. He will probably be able to show you an old logging road or route to

get to the site and give good advice as to the best building site. Good cabin sites are seldom good farmland, and costs should be low if you go off the beaten path.

2. If you are near developed lakes country you can obtain descriptive circulars as to special features of each lake, with the price of water-view sites. Most of these real estate developments are restricted as to type of structure and sometimes as to minimum cost. Depending on the location and modern improvements available, some of the sites in the New Jersey lakes district may cost as much as $3,500. If desired, the real estate company or club, if it is a cooperative project, will arrange for an architect and build any size and kind of log cabin that you want to pay for. Many of these modern summer homes represent an investment of $7,500 and are suitable for year-round homes.

3. If you are near a state park or national forest you can apply for a cabin permit from the forest service. Visit the proposed site and then call on the supervisor or forest ranger and ask him if this proposed site is available. He may want to visit the site with you or he may know it well and be able to tell from his map whether it is restricted. If not, you can fill out a permit application, stating the use to be made of the site (whether for summer camp or year-round cabin), and the cost of the improvements you intend to make; the minimum is $500, including labor. Permits are granted in the order of their receipt and the cost is low, averaging about $15 a year. Each permit is renewable annually, and the cabin must be used at least 15 days a year. With the permission of the forest service you can sell your cabin at any time.

4. Call on real estate dealers in the town nearest the location you want and find out if they know of a good camp site near the spot you are interested in. They may know of a summer-home colony on a lake where electric lights, good water, and a sewage system are available, as well as good roads for easy access and egress. They will probably know of any log cabins

or summer homes for sale and be able to quote a price. They can usually show a photograph of the property and if you look like a live prospect they will take time off to show you this and other near-by properties and sites.

5. Buy a copy of the weekly paper in a near-by town or county seat and look over the "For Sale" ads. You may find what you are looking for at a bargain price. If not, you can leave a small deposit for the insertion of a "want ad" of your own, letting it run in several issues, preferably in the fall or winter.

CHOOSING A SITE

Before selecting the site for a log cabin make up your mind whether it is to be a permanent or temporary structure. If permanent, pick a spot where there is shade during the hottest part of the day. If on a hillside, note whether the drainage flows over your site. A stone wall or drainage ditch will have to be built above the cabin to guard against water damage under such conditions. If the site is a stony knoll the foundation will have to be properly keyed into the rock so frost will not crack the foundation. Note the distance to the nearest water supply and to the road. Packing water and supplies up a hill on a hot day can become very tedious.

Men who like the idea of sitting on a back porch and casting a line into a lake in the hope of hooking fish for dinner may want a cabin built to overhang the water. If they have a motorboat or rowboat they may wish to store it in a boathouse under the cabin. For this, a substantial foundation built well into the lake bottom is essential. Posts or piers should be of stone or concrete.

Elevated ground away from swampy terrain is usually suitable. If near a lake or stream, filtered water can be obtained from a hole in the sand about 20 feet from shore, or a well can be driven to the water level with a maul and a pump installed.

Fire hazards should be taken into consideration in choosing

the site. Grass and shrubbery should not be too close to the cabin because of possible brush fires in dry weather. Log cabin insurance comes high.

In case you are building in snow country find out how deep the snow gets in the winter; if on a steep hillside note whether there have been snow slides or avalanches. For heavy snows the roof will have to be steep and reinforced for strength. A winter camp in the hills should face the south so as to get the benefit of winter sunshine. It should be below the brow of a hill and backed by a windbreak or stand of timber to protect it from the north winds.

If your location is near the seashore don't buy too close to the water. In heavy winter storms the waves roll far up on the land. The winds from summer storms may become of gale force so there should be a hill or timber between the cabin and the sea to serve as a windbreak.

If there are large boulders on the proposed site they are not too much of a handicap. They can be drilled into and blasted apart or given the fire treatment. Waste slashings are piled on the boulder and set fire to on a cold day. The frost in the boulder and the heat from the outside will start fissures. When the boulder cools a large maul can be used to break it up. Such stone cannot be used for foundations but will serve as filler.

The best site on a river is usually on a bend. Brush can be cut off to allow for the breeze, which usually flows along a valley and which keeps away mosquitoes. Clearing away the brush and a few trees will also usually add to the charm of the view.

If you want a basement or a garage for the automobile under the cabin do not select a rocky site. The cost of blasting out a cellar is very expensive.

If a real estate dealer is helping you select a site don't be swayed too much by his enthusiasm. He is thinking of his commission on the sale and is likely to be just as enthusiastic over any other site that involves the same amount of commission. Take your time and get the opinion of other members of the family or of your partners. The more people who view the site, the more opinions you will get, and no site will suit everybody.

Use your own common sense. Pick a site that will combine the best features and will make summer living as easy as possible.

Chapter 4

TOOLS

NECESSARY TOOLS

An axe is essential to get the tree to the ground, and it can be used also to trim off large limbs, though a small hand axe should be used to trim the small limbs.

Squaring off the logs can be accomplished with an axe to kerf the cut. The log is then trimmed off to the desired line with an adze. The adze may be a regular framer's adze having a hammer face, or a lip adze used by wood shipwrights.

A large two-man hand saw or a single-handed saw should be used for cutting the logs to their proper length. Chain-saws and gasoline driven power saws are used for this type of work, but such items as these would be too expensive if bought with the intention of selling after constructing one cabin.

A 7-point-to-the-inch hand-saw is necessary for coarse work such as cutting rough lumber and small logs. A 9-point-to-the-inch hand-saw is used for trim and fine work as it will not tear the sawcut as a coarse-toothed saw will.

One of the most essential tools is a carpenter's hammer for the nailing of all trim and wood-work.

A heavy 8-pound steel maul is used for driving in the steel drift pins, which are $\frac{1}{2}$ inch or $\frac{5}{8}$ inch in diameter, and vary in length from 15 to 20 inches. A hole for the drift pin or dowel should be bored through the top log at its regular size while the hole in the log below is drilled $\frac{1}{16}$ inch smaller. If soft wood, such as pine, spruce or western fir is used, the hole can be smaller, and sometimes no hole at all is necessary, the lower log being driven into by sheer force. It is not advisable to force a drift pin into oak, ash, maple, birch, or other similar hard woods without first drilling. The results may be very disappointing because the drift pin may bend and be of no use. The drift pins can be made of plain iron rods cut with a hack saw or they can be heated, cut off with a cold chisel, and pointed while still hot.

A framing chisel and wooden mallet are necessary for mortising. An axe is used for the deeper cuts.

A set of gimlet bits is useful for drilling holes for screws or spikes in hard wood. Drills or long wormed car bits, having a square shank to fit a hand brace, are another necessity. For greater power in drilling the large holes, the brace should have a long sweep on it. A wood drill shank can be welded to an iron rod and shaped like a ship auger. The brace which holds the shank of the drill in its chuck should have a large swing to give it more power when using it in hard wood. For drilling larger holes a double handle is needed such as that used for a post auger.

Countersinks are used for setting heads of screws, bolts or spikes flush with the surface and can be had in all sizes.

A draw knife can be used for cleaning the bark off logs.

For fitting of large logs a 3-inch slick is useful. The slick is a large broad heavy chisel, 2 feet or more long. This is not struck with a mallet, but pushed by the hand. To turn the logs over when fitting, a peavey or cant hook should be used as greater control by leverage can be employed in handling the logs.

When laying brick or stone for a chimney or foundation, a brick trowel is used to place the mortar between the joints. To flatten out the cement work a cement trowel is used. Always clean these tools off every day to prevent them from rusting or caking, as only tools in good condition are worth using.

It may take a novice a little time to handle various tools,

but practice makes perfect, and neat workmanship can be done by a beginner who has the proper tools, kept in good condition. *(Figs. 26–35.)*

TREE CALIPER

A tree is measured approximately 8 inches above the ground to obtain the standard measuring width. This device *(fig. 36)* can be made of wood or metal and used to measure any tree from 3 inches to 12 inches in diameter. This is an important gadget when building a log cabin, as a tree of the proper size is necessary.

SHARPENING WOODEN BITS

When sharpening wooden bits a little knowledge of the bit is helpful. For drilling in hard wood it becomes necessary to have a fine thread or worm, but on soft wood a heavy thread can be used. If a power drill is used driven by electricity or air, the worm should be removed with a file by squaring or rounding the point. The lips should be kept sharp, and when power drilling be sure to lift the drill out to remove the chips occasionally. Otherwise they will build up behind the drill worm and freeze the drill in the hole. This will cause delay in work in removing the drill. When sharpening the drill, file the upper side of the cutting surface, using a fine file—a regular drill file, if possible. *(Fig. 37.)*

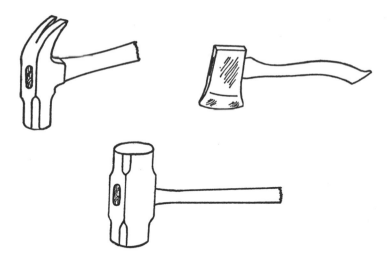

Fig. 26 *Upper left,* Heavy Claw Hammer; *upper right,* Hand Hatchet; *lower,* 8-Pound Maul

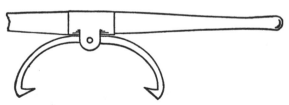

Fig. 27 Timber Carrier or Lughook

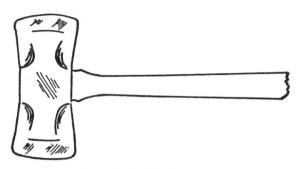

Fig. 28 Double Faced Axe

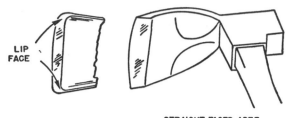

STRAIGHT FACED ADZE

Fig. 29

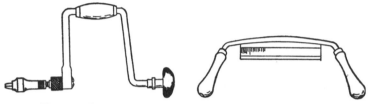

Fig. 30 *Left,* Brace with 14″ Sweep; *right,* Draw Knife

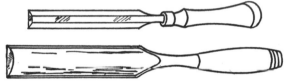

Fig. 31 *Upper,* ¾-inch Wood Chisel; *lower,* Framing Chisel

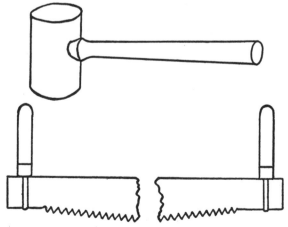

Fig. 32 *Upper,* Wooden Mallet; *lower,* Two-Man Saw

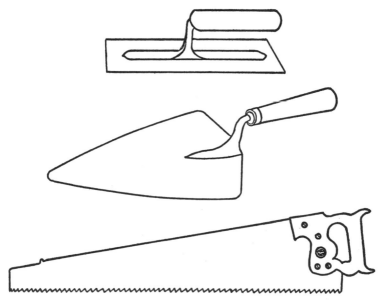

Fig. 33 *Upper*, Cement Trowel; *center*, Brick Trowel; *lower*, Hand Cross-Cut Saw (7 Point)

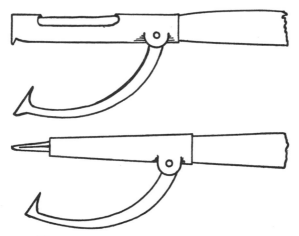

Fig. 34 *Upper*, Cant Hook; *lower*, Peavey

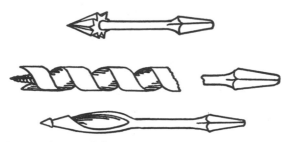

Fig. 35   *Upper,* Countersink; *center,* Long Car-Bits; *lower,* Gimlet Bit

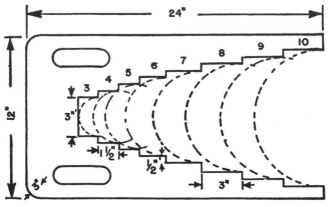

Fig. 36   Tree Caliper

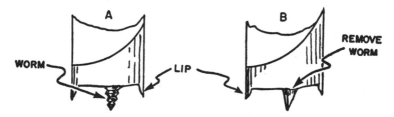

Fig. 37   Sharpening Bits: A, for Hand Drilling; B, for Power Drilling

Chapter 5

AVAILABLE TIMBER ON PROPERTY

When building a log cabin it is advisable to build it where timber is plentiful. A person buying five acres of wooded ground should not expect to secure enough timber from that property to build a large cabin. Cut logs may be purchased from neighbors and delivered to the property for a price anywhere from $.50 to $2.00 a log, depending on the wood and length. Or the neighbor may sell trees which can be felled and hauled away at a price that depends on how badly the neighbor wants to get rid of his timber; it may be had for nothing and then again for approximately $.50 to $2.50 per tree. Good sharp sand should be available on the property. If it is not, it could be purchased and delivered to the site for from $1.50 to $3.00 a cubic yard.

Stone that can be picked up from a field and used without having to quarry it will save a great deal of time. If the cabin is built near a stream the backbreaking work of pumping for water supply can be avoided. Trucking material over good roads is important and should be considered not only for supplying building material but for the home supply after the cabin is finished.

The timber should be approximately 8 inches in diameter after it has been peeled of the bark. It should be a variety that is easy to work if this is a first attempt at building a cabin. Pine, spruce, hemlock and tamarack are soft woods and easy to work.

HANDLING LOGS

Building a log cabin does not entail a great deal of ingenuity on the part of the builder, but more or less common sense. Our forefathers were by no means builders, most of them being farmers who made their living from the good earth, some depending more and some less on their inventive genius and progressiveness. With better tools now available, and with sketches as shown in this book, a novice can build a cabin of any of the many styles and types here shown and illustrated.

One of the objects to bear in mind is that when one is handling heavy timbers he must use special caution to avoid accidents to himself or his helpers. If guy ropes are used in lifting the timbers in place, never use old rope, and beware of timbers swung overhead. In rolling the timbers into place and also in notching them, a peavey or cant hook is used as either will give good leverage in swinging or turning the timbers. The scaffold on which the worker must stand and work must be strong enough to hold not only the worker but the timbers that are being worked, and it must be strongly braced to avoid any swaying or movement.

When handling an adze the handle should be grasped firmly with both hands, keeping the elbow against the body at about waist height. In swinging the adze use the elbow point as a hinge and if a clean cut is desired hold in position so that the adze cuts slightly diagonal to the grain of the wood. If the adze is swung with the grain of the log it is apt to dig too deeply, and if swung directly crosswise the cut is apt to be less smooth. When using the adze for cutting knots in timbers, the knot must be cut by hitting its center with the center of the cutting edge of the adze. When cutting large wood chunks or when dressing logs, a broad axe should be used to kerf the log surface and to rough it to the desired size. Finishing is done with an adze or plane depending on how smooth a surface is wanted.

MOST SUITABLE TYPES OF TIMBER

The timber most suitable for log cabins is not always available in all parts of the country. For instance, practically nothing but heavy yellow pitch pine grows in Louisiana and Texas. Yellow pine is a suitable wood and easy to cut, but it is so saturated with pitch that it is very difficult to make creosote penetrate it.

Oak is a hard wood to work, especially white oak, but a cabin built of it will stand for many years. Red oak is also a suitable wood and can be saturated with preservatives to make it last a long time. Working with red oak is somewhat easier than with white oak.

Hemlock and tamarack are easy woods to work but also readily affected by the sun and weather and need many applications of wood preservatives for a long durable life.

Southern cedar is not available in the large log sizes necessary for cabins though it would be suitable for furniture.

Pine of the northern variety is suitable and very easy to work, and when properly stained and maintained makes an ideal wood. Spruce and fir can also be classified as good wood for use in building cabins and are likewise easy to work.

Birch, poplar, and willow can be used, but have a short life and need special care and treatment for cabin walls. These woods can be used in building inside partitions and furniture. Cypress is good for a swampy location.

Maple, ash, hickory and beech are hard woods that are difficult to work, but the cabin wall built of these will last indefinitely and require very little care.

No matter how good any log looked in the bark, or how badly it is needed, it should not be used if full of destructive insects as it will contaminate other logs. The cost of getting rid of insects will be more than the log is worth. Such wood is good only for firewood.

THINGS TO REMEMBER

When building your log cabin set your goal and stick to it. Friends' advice may help you, but you may change your mind as to whether their advice was worth taking. Build your cabin within your means—do not try to keep up with the Jones's who may have the means to build with professional help. If you have a car, place your cabin on a site that will not make it necessary to park it a long distance from the cabin. Cut a roadway into the cabin site, avoiding marshy water holes. If the road must cross such a space, corduroy the roadway with log and limb cuttings. Since you need a large water supply and food for a cabin, these commodities must be close by. Food can be raised and brought in and stored. The author remembers that when he was a child his grandparents stored milk in cold running springs that had a sunken box large enough to hold the high galvanized milk cans. Wood can be cut for fuel but must be dried before using unless it comes from dead trees which may have been cut to clear the woods.

Chapter 6

CLEARING THE SITE

FELLING TREES

When cutting down trees in the woods one naturally prefers to cut them in the manner that requires the least amount of work and time. The tree can be made to fall in the direction you want it to—if it does not lean too much in the opposite direction—by making the first cut at right angles to the falling direction. Make the first cut as shown in "A" *(fig. 38)* a little beyond the middle of the tree, cutting with a downward swing, then cut from the lower side with a slightly upward cut on the alternating swing. When you have progressed a little beyond the middle of the tree, commence on the second cut on the opposite side as shown in "B."

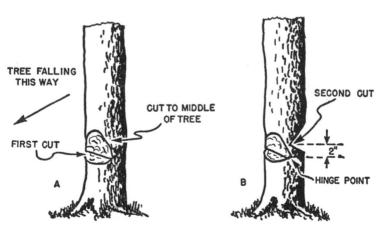

Fig. 38   Felling Trees

An experienced woodsman makes the first cut with a saw until the saw starts to jam, then pulls out the saw and cuts with the axe until he has cut to a ring line beyond the center point of the tree. He then saws on the other side about two inches above the first cut until the tree starts to fall. He retrieves the saw, steps about eight feet away opposite the falling side of the tree, and as the tree falls where he wanted it to, he gets satisfaction in his workmanship.

HOLDING A TREE WHEN FELLING

If a tree is leaning as shown in "D" (fig. 39), it will always fall in the direction that it is leaning unless it is held back or

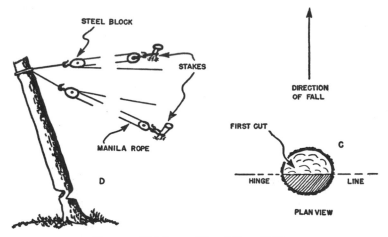

Fig. 39   Holding a Tree When Felling

forced back by rope lines. If rope lines are used to prevent the tree from falling in a space where it would cause some damage, the method is recommended, otherwise it is common sense to let it fall where it may.

"C" shows a plan view of the hinge line and the direction a tree should fall.

BEAVER CUT

The beaver cut *(fig. 40)* is an example of the wrong way to fell a tree for the direction the tree falls cannot be anticipated, so it may fall on the workman and cause bodily harm. Old beavers cut trees up to four inches in diameter and even larger, and commence on the side facing the water, if the lake or stream is near by, to let the tree fall in the lake if possible. This uncertain method should not be used by human beings.

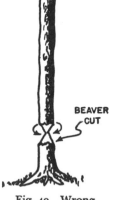

BEAVER CUT

Fig. 40   Wrong Method

HILLSIDE TREE FELLING

When felling trees on a hill do not stand on the lower side of the slope where the tree is to fall. Be sure there are no loose stones or twigs around the tree roots that may cause you to slip as you back away from the tree when it starts to fall. Do not forget that if the slope is steep the tree will end up at the bottom regardless of its distance from the bottom. *(Fig. 41.)*

GRUBBING STUMPS

Removing tree stumps from a cut-over section of land, lawn or yard is a problem to one with no experience. If the ground is soft and you desire to remove stumps with a stump-puller, it is better to leave about 4 feet of stump standing above the ground to give a better hold. Tie the stump-puller near the base of two or more stumps or a live tree, and then tie the stump-puller cable to the stump to be removed. As the stump-puller is tightened and starts to force the stump over, cut the roots with a grub axe until the stump is free from the ground. Stump roots should be cut off as deep in the ground as possible to prevent sprouts from coming to the surface again.

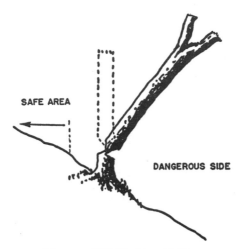

SAFE AREA

DANGEROUS SIDE

Fig. 41   Hillside Tree Felling

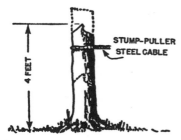

STUMP-PULLER
STEEL CABLE

4 FEET

Fig. 42   Cutting for Stump-
Pulling Machine

If no stump-puller is used the choice of cutting the stump in line with the surface of the ground or digging it up must be made. When digging up a tree stump, a great deal of hard work is necessary to cut around the roots and pull the stump out. The hole could be filled with rubbish, then topped with black soil on which grass can be grown. To make the fill settle readily, water when filling, and when it dries out the dirt will have filled every crevice in the ground. *(Fig. 42.)*

DESTROYING STUMPS

A method of chemically destroying tree stumps is illustrated in *fig. 43*. When the stump is dry, drill a hole 1½ inches in diameter and 6 inches or more deep into the heartwood or center of the stump (see "A"). Pour 4 tablespoonfuls of saltpeter and a little water into the hole. Close the hole with sawdust or rotted bark and let this stand until the following year. When the weather is favorable, clean out the hole, fill it with kerosene, and then set the stump on fire. To hasten the procedure, bore 1-inch holes around the stump as at "B" and

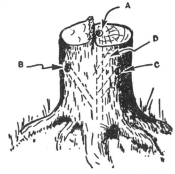

Fig. 43   Destroying Stumps

"C" into the heartwood. When the stump is ablaze, throw in scrap twigs to burn with the stump to make a good strong fire.

REMOVING LARGE BOULDERS

If large boulders are to be removed from the property with little or no effort, the following method is best employed.

Fig. 44   Removing Large Boulders

Place all the scrap material that will burn on and around the boulder. Then, on the coldest winter day set fire to the scrap, the bigger the fire, the better. When this has cooled, take an 8-pound stone maul and proceed to demolish the boulder. The moisture in the boulder, plus the heat, will have cracked the stone in a thousand places, and breaking will be an easy task. Because of the large number of cracks in these stones, they should not be used for a foundation, but only for fill or road making purposes. *(Fig. 44.)*

Chapter 7

BUILDING PREPARATION

HOLDING LOGS FOR DRESSING

When logs are being dressed they can be held by steel dogs which are driven into the log itself and the two logs upon which they rest. If the log is a long one it will become

Fig. 45   Holding Logs for Dressing

necessary to place more than two logs for it to rest on. Use a log straight edge to line up the surface and a broad axe for kerfing, with an adze for dressing. If a perfectly smooth surface is wanted use a jack plane. Time can be saved by sending the logs to a mill. *(Fig. 45.)*

TRIMMING TIMBERS

When hewing a flat surface on a timber, make kerf cuts along the timber to the desired line and then trim to the surface with an adze, using either a straight or lip adze. Care should be taken in handling an adze, especially when cutting around a knot, as the adze may fly out of control if not held firmly, and cause the user bodily harm. *(Fig. 46.)*

Fig. 46   Trimming Timbers

STRIPPING LOGS

All furniture or wood used in a camp should be stripped of its bark. This is done by peeling with a chisel or draw knife, or in some cases boiling the log in water which loosens

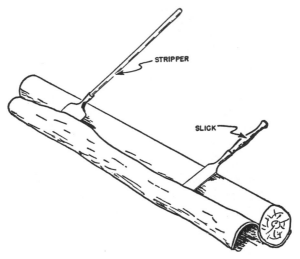

Fig. 47   Stripping of Log

the bark so that it peels very easily. The peeled log or sapling should have a coat or a mixture of 1 gallon of creosote to 3 gallons of kerosene applied with a brush, by spraying, or by dipping if possible. This material will penetrate into the wood and prevent tree borers from damaging the wood. The same can be applied to furniture which can then be sandpapered and varnished. Linseed oil mixed with turpentine has been widely used for a finish. One quart of linseed oil and one quart of turpentine are mixed and applied with a brush or cloth. The dark skin of the wood under the bark should be removed to give it a lighter finish. This can be taken off with a wood scraper and sandpaper. *(Fig. 47.)*

Chapter 8

FOUNDATIONS

The foundation for a log cabin is the first and most important thing to consider. If the log cabin is built in a cold climate and the frost penetrates deep into the ground, the building will be affected by the frost, unless the foundation has been made correctly. In this case the foundation should be as deep as the penetration of the frost, say about 3 feet, so as to prevent any movement of the building when the ground thaws and softens. Movement in the building causes cracks

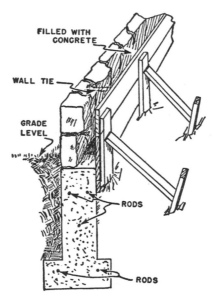

FILLED WITH CONCRETE

WALL TIE

GRADE LEVEL

RODS

RODS

Fig. 48   Concrete Wall with Small Footing

in chinking, etc. A 12-inch wide foundation reinforced with five ½-inch diameter pickled steel rods placed as shown in *fig. 48* will be sufficient to prevent the foundation from cracking or pulling apart. After filling the trench with concrete to the grade level, a facing of quarry stone or cobblestone is put in. Wall ties are then placed between the joints so that they protrude into what will be the concrete fill in the back of the foundation.

The stone facing should have ½-inch space left between each stone for mortar and each stone should be free from moss, scale, etc. To clean the stone a wooden-handled steel brush is useful. If you are fortunate enough to build near a creek where there are plenty of clean free stones, the task will be easily done by leaving the dirty stones in the current until ready for use.

The foundation back-fill mixture should be 1 part cement, 3 parts sand, and 4 parts pebbles or crushed stone, by volume, using a bucket, for example, as a measuring unit. Small stones no larger than an egg should be used as larger ones will weaken the wall. The larger stones should be saved for the foundation facing, fireplace and chimney. An abundance of stone gives a greater variety and a much more satisfactory job. Stone can always be used around a cabin. After the facing has been constructed, a board form is put in place for the backing of the foundation and braced securely, filling in with concrete with two rows of reinforcing rods and fill.

RAKED JOINT

This illustration *(fig. 49)* of stone work shows a flush joint and a raked joint. In the former the mortar or cement is flush with the surface of the stone. The raked joint is one in which the mortar has been cut out with a raking tool. The raking tool is made of wood, with a cut-out slot and a 10-penny nail driven into it, the head being left about ¼

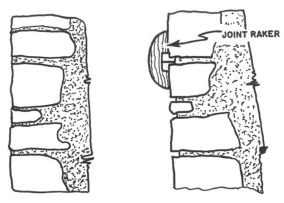

Fig. 49   Masonry Joints: *left,* Flush Joint; *right,* Raked Joint

inch beyond the guide surface. The joint raker should be passed all around the joint so that it cleans out the mortar. The joint is then troweled smooth with a joint iron that is thin enough to get into the joint.

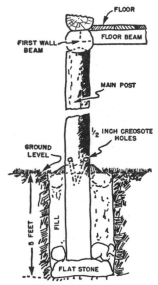

Fig. 50   Supporting Post

SUPPORTING POST

It is not difficult to build a cabin which rests on posts. The posts should be approximately 12 inches in diameter, stripped of their bark and soaked in creosote. In creosoting so large a timber a block and fall tied to the limb of a tree about 12 feet off the ground will be needed. Put a timber hitch from the block and fall around the middle of the post, and raise it enough so it can be lowered into a barrel of creosote which is placed directly under it. Keep a strain on the block and fall by tying the rope to a tree, otherwise the post will tip the barrel over and spill the creosote on the ground. Set the posts in first and then fill the barrel with creosote. This method will prevent the creosote from spilling over the barrel.

Place a flat stone as a footing in the hole which is about 5 feet deep. Now lower the posts into the hole, place stones around the bottom, and fill with earth. Next place stones around the top and drill about three holes ½ inch in diameter to the heartwood, which is the center of the post. About twice a year fill these holes with creosote, and brush the rest of the creosote on the post. If the cabin is placed in swampland, the creosoting should be applied more often. *(Fig. 50.)*

BONDING IN MASONRY

Bonding in masonry refers to the method of lapping stone joints as shown at "A" *(fig. 51)*. This is the best method of holding the stones in place. Properly bonded stone masonry

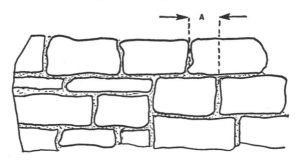

Fig. 51   Bonding of Field Stone Masonry

is strong and neat in appearance. Fireplaces, foundations and retaining walls made of stone should be well bonded and firmly set.

STOCKADE-BUILT CABIN

This foundation is a puddle footing around the bottom end of the stockade outside slabs. This can best be accomplished by erecting the corner posts first, plumbing them up with braces and filling the rest in later. The concrete outside sill is added after the wood has completely dried. The floor is a 3-inch slab of concrete placed over a tamped

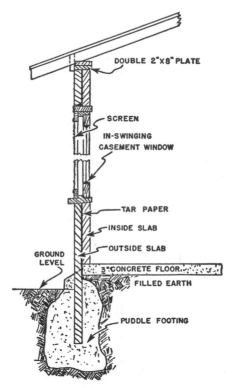

DOUBLE 2"x8" PLATE

SCREEN

IN-SWINGING
CASEMENT WINDOW

TAR PAPER

INSIDE SLAB

OUTSIDE SLAB

GROUND
LEVEL

3" CONCRETE FLOOR

FILLED EARTH

PUDDLE FOOTING

Fig. 52   Section of Stockade Cabin

earth fill. A double plate is placed on the top to keep the wall straight and receive the roof rafters. This type of cabin is best built in a location where the ground is fairly level or has a slight slope. The calking on top of the window header should be made of calking compound to prevent water from seeping into the house over the window. The window could be fitted in after the long lengths of the wall are up, cutting the short lengths later between the windows. The windows should be uniformly spaced between the joints to give a more attractive appearance. *(Fig. 52.)*

PIERS TO HOLD LOG CABIN

If the cabin must be set on piers to raise it off the ground, or if piers are placed on one side, preparations must be made

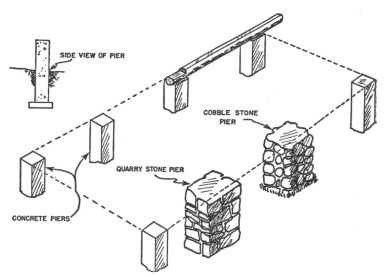

Fig. 53   Various Types of Piers

so the piers will be strong enough to carry the weight above them. If concrete piers are used, they should be not less than 16 x 16 inches square and placed into the ground to a depth below the frost line, usually about 3 feet. The spans between piers should not be over 12 feet and the tops of all piers should be on the same level. If quarry stone is used, the piers should not be less than 18 x 18 inches square and well bonded with a good grade of stone. The cobblestone or quarry stone pier should be at least 20 x 20 inches square, and must be tied together with wire and rods imbedded in the mortar. These tie rods prevent cracking and checking of the piers, which, if allowed to start, can only be remedied by rebuilding completely. (*Fig. 53.*)

KEYING A FOUNDATION INTO A HILLSIDE

The foundation for a log cabin depends upon the type of cabin to be built and on the location. Foundations can be

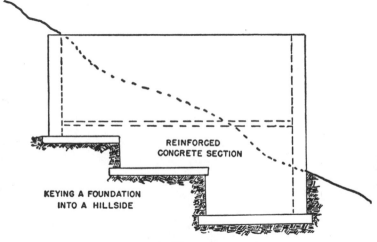

REINFORCED
CONCRETE SECTION

KEYING A FOUNDATION
INTO A HILLSIDE

Fig. 54

made of cobblestone or concrete. A cobblestone foundation without reinforcing rods is apt to crack or be heaved by frost. Cobblestone should have wall ties placed between the joints at 16-inch intervals to prevent cracking, or be backed up with a concrete back facing. There should be plenty of free cobblestones on the premises. Quarry stone makes a neat foundation but would be rather expensive if the individual had to quarry the stone himself.

Posts set into the ground should be steeped in creosote for a week to saturate them thoroughly, and the ends should also be plastered with an asphaltic cement so that the timber eating wood insects will be kept from these supporting posts indefinitely. A large flat rock or a cement footing approximately 3 feet square should be placed underneath the post.

Concrete foundations made in the form of a wall or piers can be used, but must be 14 inches thick if built as a wall and 16 inches square if placed in piers. Good sand and stones no larger than the size of half an egg should be used in the concrete wall. If a concrete wall is built over a stone slope it must be keyed to the slope by iron rods or offsets, as shown (*fig. 54*), in the stone or earth, otherwise the cabin is apt to move down the slope.

Chapter 9

WALLS

Very few trees are the same diameter at the ground level as on the top where the branches start to grow. So, when building a cabin, the manner of stacking the logs in the wall is important. The log ends should be reversed, if the thickness varies, the top of the first being placed on one end of the building and the top end of the next at the other end. They should be kept as uniform in size as possible—not ranging from a 6-inch to

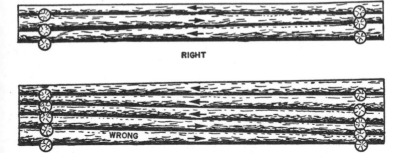

Fig. 55   Keeping Wall Logs Level

a 10-inch log. Neither is it advisable to place two or three logs together with their smaller ends on one end of the building and then reverse the next two or three with the smaller diameters to the other end, as it shows a haphazard method of building. If the size of the timbers seems to vary a great deal, it will be advisable to use the larger timbers closer to the ground, gradually reducing the size of the logs used as the top is approached. (*Fig. 55.*)

SPACING BETWEEN LOGS

Bracing the logs to avoid sagging before chinking and settling is important. Do not permit the spacing between the logs to be too great on long spans as this is apt to cause sagging or springing movement. Where there is spacing such as is caused by sagging, wedge the log up to a straight line. Keep the wedges between the logs permanently, chinking around them. Slamming of doors will cause the chinking to fall out if it has not been properly keyed and if the logs have not been wedged.

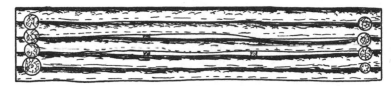

Fig. 56   Spacing between Logs

Large chinking can be filled with white Portland cement, or Portland cement mixed with slacked lime, after the space has been calked with oakum. Carefully fitted squared logs can be chinked with a putty calking compound after first calking them with oakum. *(Fig. 56.)*

SHINGLES OVER THE DORMER

The dormer of a cabin can be boarded and shingled to make an inexpensive but good appearing side of the building. The boards are nailed to uprights and the shingles are nailed to the rough boards after a tar paper has been put on. *(Figs. 57 and 58.)*

DORMER CONSTRUCTION

A dormer continued up the side wall makes a pleasing appearance but provision must be made to support the inner end of the dormer by a cross beam extending to each side of

Fig. 57   Framing Dormer

Fig. 58   Shingled Dormer Side

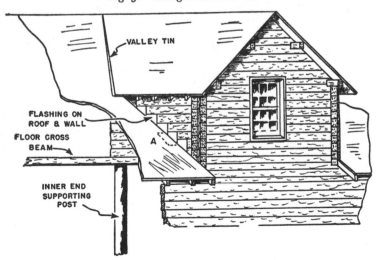

VALLEY TIN

FLASHING ON
ROOF & WALL

FLOOR CROSS
BEAM

A

INNER END
SUPPORTING
POST

Fig. 59   Dormer Construction

the cabin and one on each side of the dormer. The floor cross beam is supported by a post under the end. The footing must be of stone to prevent the cross timber from settling. The flashing should be made to prevent rain from entering between the wall and roof. It must extend up the joint of the logs and be bent so the flashing will lay along the roof underneath the shingles for approximately 6 inches, as shown at "A" (*fig. 59*).

BUILDING LOG CABIN WALLS

The walls are preferably built from long straight logs. If some slightly curved logs must be used, they should not be placed as shown in "A" (*fig. 60*), as this will produce a bulge

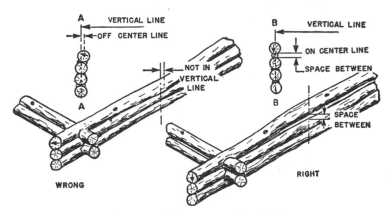

Fig. 60   Building Log Cabin Walls

and give the wall an unsightly appearance. Instead, the log should be turned so that the bulge is in the wall line as shown at "B." The opening between the logs can then be calked with oakum and cement. If the log is bent too much it is better to cut into shorter straight lengths.

SCAFFOLDING WHEN BUILDING

When building a log cabin a fair degree of common sense is needed to avoid a great amount of unnecessary lifting and to insure safety. Logs are not easy to handle; they are heavy and cumbersome. The work of raising walls can be made simpler by building a scaffold around the outside of the building. Plan the scaffold uprights high enough to allow work to be done

Fig. 61   Scaffolding While Building

easily at the top of the dormer or roof. The first height of the scaffold is about 4 feet, or window-sill height. The next scaffold height is the top of the windows, as shown (*fig. 61*), and if a greater height is desired, the scaffold might be placed at about 4-foot intervals. The uprights should never be less than five inches in diameter, and the cross braces of 1-inch thick boards should be about 8 to 10 inches wide, nailed to the building uprights at each end with 8-penny common nails. If there is no planking available to walk on, 6-inch logs can be used but must be dressed so they will not roll. These should be bolted together with a crosswise 2- by 6-inch plank at the center of the span so they will hold each other in place if greater weight is placed on one of them.

SPLICING

Splicing a log is a small matter, but the splices should be kept as far away from each other as possible. Try to keep the logs that are to be spliced the same size at the point of splicing, or trim the larger log to conform with the small log end. Place the large dowels so there are two in the splice and one on each side beyond the splice, as shown. (*Fig. 62.*) Drill the hole so

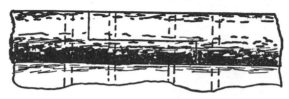

Fig. 62   Splicing Logs

that it penetrates at least 4 inches into the log under the spliced log. Timbers that are properly spliced so that no calking is needed on the butt end make a better appearance.

CHINKING

Chinking is the means by which the logs, where fastened together, can be made watertight. Oakum can be placed in between the logs after the wall has been built, or at the time of laying them. If wire lath instead of oakum is placed in the wall while the wall is being built, it will be difficult to do chinking against the wire. When the logs are all sized and a small joint is visible, it is best to chink with oakum and fill with calking compound with a gun. By this method a small neat joint can be made which will be absolutely watertight as well as insect-tight.

SPLINED CHINKING

If immediate occupancy is desired the splined chinking method may be employed. This method, however, makes it necessary to have the splines cut out and logs surfaced at a mill. The logs are surfaced on two sides and then two 1 inch by 1 inch hardwood splines nailed to the top surfaced sides of the logs as shown (*fig. 63*), and a ½ inch by 1 inch on the bottom surface. The logs should be marked on the side, op-

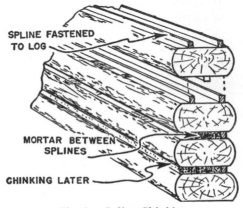

SPLINE FASTENED
TO LOG

MORTAR BETWEEN
SPLINES

CHINKING LATER

Fig. 63   Spline Chinking

posite the points where nails are driven into the under spline so as to prevent drilling into the nails. Fresh mortar cement is poured between the two splines on the top surface and the next log dropped in place.

As the splines dry out, the log rests firmly on the concrete. Chinking of both the outside and inside of the wall can be done later. If the cabin is to be used as a winter home, the calking of a few cracks will be necessary to keep snow and rain out.

The reason for the 1 inch by 1 inch square spline on top and the ½ inch by 1 inch on the bottom is that, when the log is lowered onto the under-log, the center bottom spline will be forced into the concrete deep enough to help lock the log in place but not so far that it will prevent the top log from resting on the two splines on the under-log. If the center spline is the same height, the cement resting under the center spline will prevent the log from resting firmly on the upper two splines.

The cement should be fairly wet so there will be no trouble in forcing the log down. A slight striking by a large wooden maul will help to force the center spline into the cement. Splines and flat surfaces of logs should be creosoted before installing in the wall. It must be borne in mind that the log should fit properly with the splines fastened properly before rolling back for cementing.

WIRE LATH FOR CHINKING

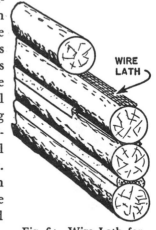

Galvanized wire lath placed in between the logs for chinking when "walling up" (slang for building the wall), saves chinking time but makes drilling for drift pins or trunnels more difficult. This can be overcome by first drilling with the wood drill to a safe distance and then finishing by drilling the remainder of the required distance with a steel drill which has a long shank welded to it. This method is better for barns than for homes, as the chinking may not be watertight unless oakum is first placed into the joint. If oakum is placed underneath, and wire lath placed on top,

Fig. 64 Wire Lath for Chinking

it requires an excellent mechanic to calk the oakum without affecting the lath for the outside chinking. *(Fig. 64.)*

WHEN TO CHINK

Chinking should be done after the logs have dried out. This usually takes a summer's airing unless the logs were cut and dried a year before. If one builds a log cabin in the summer and fells his trees when the leaves are green, he should peel and build his cabin in order to have a shelter as soon

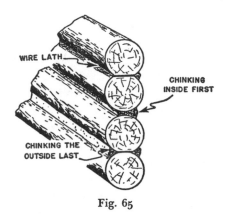

Fig. 65

as possible. It is true that trees cut more easily when they are green, but the finished cabin will not be as satisfactory if built from green timber, because of shrinkage and checking. If a rush for shelter is the primary objective, the chinking should be done on the inside first to keep out mosquitoes, insects, and rain. The inside chinking does not necessarily need to be finished; merely close the cracks and finish later on. The outside should be done after the logs have been cleaned and dried. Any cracks can be filled with calking compounds, using a calking gun or stick. *(Fig. 65.)*

CALKING METHOD

Considerable construction time will be saved if oakum padding is tacked to the log at the time the log is placed in the wall. The width of the strip should be governed by the diameter of the logs. If 6-inch logs are used, a 2-inch padding would be suitable, and if 10-inch logs use a 4-inch padding. This

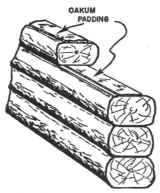

Fig. 66   Calking Method

should be tacked into place, keeping the tacks to the outside and staggering them. This is done to prevent the wood drill from striking the tacks when drilling for drift rods or trunnels. (*Fig. 66.*)

LARGE SPACING BETWEEN LOGS

The spacing between the logs is not so important as one would be led to believe. If a log is not straight and touches

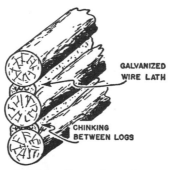

Fig. 67   Chinking Large Space between Logs

the under log here and there, with an opening up to 2 inches in another spot, the chinking can fill up the space very readily. The joints should be kept nearly uniform, and the logs, if crooked, can be made to look straight by a little straightening of the chinking joint. *(Fig. 67.)*

TYPES OF CORNERS

The methods of building corners are more or less a matter of taste. Many individuals prefer the old pioneer styles regardless of cost or time in construction. As the present-day woodmen develop the log cabins, new styles and improvements are being made that beautify and simplify the construction. Illustrations of several types of corner construction are shown.

VERTICAL SLABS

The plan view of a stockade system of building a cabin is shown in *fig. 68*. Half-round logs are used except for the quarter-round inside corner slab. Two corner slabs are nailed

Fig. 68   Vertical Slab Corner—Plan View

together at right angles and the inside corner covered with a large quarter-round slab. The half-round slabs are set vertically with flat surfaces back to back and the slabs overlapping as shown in the plan view. The logs forming the stockade wall are fastened together by drilling and countersinking for long wood screws. This prevents any movement in fitting the surfaces together. Drill a countersunk clearance hole through the first slab, and an undersize hole drilled with gimlet for the next slab so that the screw will turn easily enough to keep it from breaking. Use a brace with screw-driven bit for the screw because a better leverage can be had in forcing the screw in. Soap the screw to prevent it from sticking and fill when finished.

STOCKADE WALL WITH PLYWOOD

A stockade wall with plywood would be satisfactory for a summer house and would make a neat appearance both outside and inside. If both outside and inside of a house are to have a stockade appearance it would be an advantage to have the closets and bathroom lined with plywood rather than slabs on the inside. Plywood can be had in thicknesses of ¼ inch to ¾ inch. For an inside partition for closets and bathroom the plywood should be ½ inch thick and the vertical stockading logs should be laid out so they come over the scam of the plywood even if you have to cut the plywood.

For an outside wall a ¾-inch plywood should be used the entire height of the ceiling if possible. Plywood can be had in sheets of various thicknesses 4 feet wide and 8 to 10 feet long. If 8 feet is the longest length to be had make a neat fit and place a batten around the joint. Before placing the slab against the plywood, creosote both the plywood and slab surface.

Two-inch wood screws with countersunk heads can be used for ½-inch plywood, and 2½-inch screws for ¾-inch plywood. The screws should be placed into the stockade from the back side, that is, through the plywood, and then into the backside of the slabs. Good judgment can be used in placing the screws so they will not hit the stockade joints on the outside. A tar felt paper could be placed between the plywood and slabs to prevent seepage of rain. After the slabs have a chance to dry out the joints should be calked with calking compound with

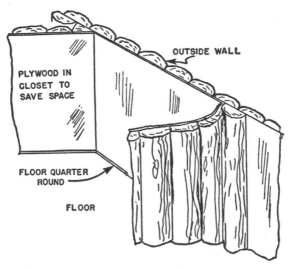

Fig. 69   Stockade Construction with Plywood

a calking gun, as the joints would not be deep enough for chinking. *(Fig. 69.)*

STOCKADE TYPE CABIN

A trench about 15 inches wide and 3 feet deep should be dug, placing the four corners of the cabin up first. Next, intermediate posts are set up, spacing them so a full slab will fit in properly. Each corner should be braced two ways and filled in between, nailing the slabs against the upper and lower braces to hold them up in the air. The tops should be fit in line with a center line on the under surface of the plate, the height being kept even with the top corner posts which should have been previously leveled. As the slabs are held free in the air, the space around the slabs should be filled in with concrete and stones, using none larger than a coconut, and keeping the inside of the wall surface straight. A section on one side should be worked, then the other, to give the concrete a chance to get hard.

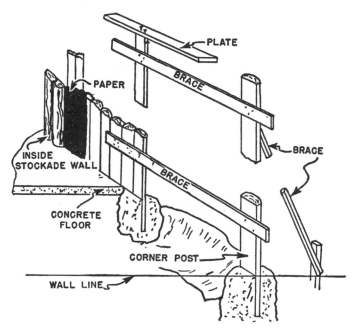

Fig. 70   Stockade Half Logs Building Method

After this outer wall of slabs is completed, the roof can be framed in but not covered. The concrete floor should be laid and then the inside slabs can be set up after a tar felt has been put on the wall. The roof can then be finished and the windows and doors set in. If an inside finish of ⅞-inch plywood is more desirable, place this on the inside after the stockade; finish and fasten the plywood to the inside of the slabs. *(Fig. 70.)*

NEW ENGLAND COLONIAL TYPE CORNERS

This style of corner is made square faced by using an adze, and all ends are approximately the same size. A small chamfer corner caused by the round surface of the log is immaterial;

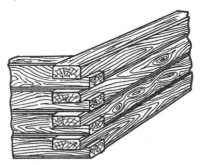

Fig. 71   New England Colonial Style Corner

in fact, it gives a pioneer effect. This particular style was built in the upper New England states and in some Midwestern states, and is a sturdy type of construction. *(Fig. 71.)*

MORTISED CORNERS

In *fig. 72* "A" shows a corner half mortised, forming a right angle, each two meeting members making a complete height.

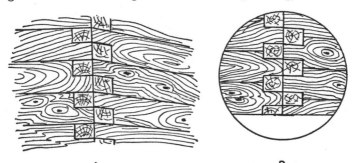

A   **B**

Fig. 72   Half and Quarter Notched Mortised Corner

"B" shows a corner mortise where the same mortise fits from either side.

To start a wall, a half log is first laid and the right angle timber is then placed over the corner. Thus the wall is continued, first one side and then the other, up to its final height.

SQUARE TIMBER CORNERS

(Fig . 73.) "A" shows the square corner dovetailed.

"B" shows a dressed square cob corner in which the ends extend approximately 8 inches beyond the wall line.

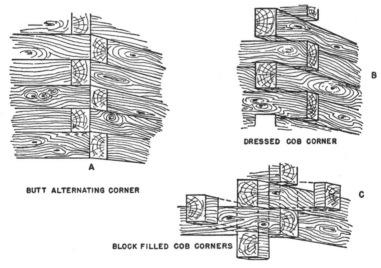

BUTT ALTERNATING CORNER

DRESSED COB CORNER

BLOCK FILLED COB CORNERS

Fig. 73 Square Timber Corners

"C" shows how cob corners can be filled up with blocks set into the corners and nailed or doweled to the other members.

MITER DOVETAIL CORNER

(Fig. 74.) "A" shows a locking dovetail corner which requires two timber heights to make a complete lock unit. The height of the wall should be an even number of timbers to have complete units.

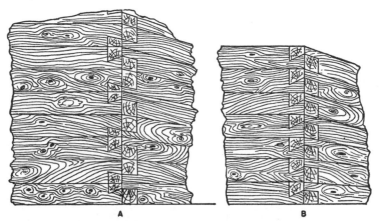

Fig. 74   Miter Dovetail Corner

"B" shows the complete dovetail on a single-height timber unit. The ends of the timber should not extend more than 1 inch beyond the side wall. If the side wall is to be colonial shingled or covered with some other surface, the ends should be cut flush with the side walls.

DOVETAIL CORNERS

In this particular corner construction, the logs have been sized at a mill and the corners laid out with templates to insure a perfect fit. By this method the logs hold themselves together at a corner, needing little or no corner spiking. A neatly constructed house of this type can be covered with siding or shingles, if the owner so desires. The corner ends should be left hanging over at least 3 inches and painted with red lead to prevent the log ends from checking, and after a year or so of drying, the ends should be cut to a

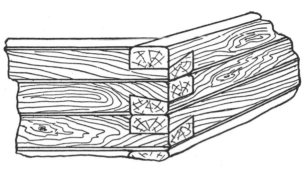

Fig. 75   Dovetail Corners

straight line. This type of corner is hardly a job for a beginner at log cabin construction, for many corners badly cut would mean a waste of labor and material. *(Fig. 75.)*

HALF MORTISE CORNER

This type of mortised corner *(fig. 76)* is the easiest and simplest to make, and yet is very practical if spiked in the proper places. The logs have all been milled and need merely be laid into place and cut out. The logs should protrude 3 inches over each end, and log "A" can be mortised out on the wall after it has been spiked or trunneled to the wall. Log "B" can be marked out and rolled back from the end with a cant hook or peavey hook which all log handlers should have. The fit between the logs should be tight and not left so the weight of the resting log will lay solely on the corner mortise. Chinking at the mortise joint can be done to the extent of ¼ inch to make up for shrinkage, but more than that would look like bad workmanship.

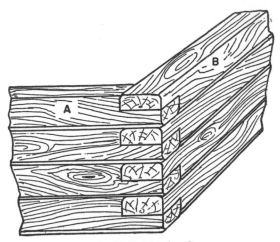

Fig. 76 Half Mortise Corner

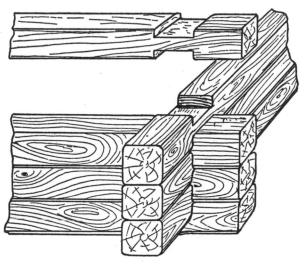

Fig. 77 Double Mortise Corner

DOUBLE MORTISE CORNER

This really can be called the only factory-made corner. *(Fig. 77.)* The logs are all sized and the corners are cut out alike at the mill. The lengths can be trucked to the job and installed with a little fitting. The mortise joints should be thoroughly saturated with creosote before laying them together to prevent insects from infesting the crevices. As the wood dries out there are bound to be crevices (called shakes) in the wood, and they should be filled with calking compound which is really a soft putty that never gets hard. Calking compound in various shades of white, light gray, black and red can be had from dealers.

COB CORNERS FOR SQUARED LOGS

This type of corner construction can be done in the woods and set up anywhere if the wall ends are the same.

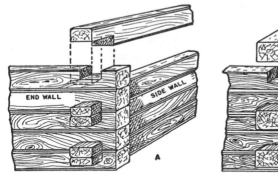

Fig. 78   One Side Cob Corner, One   One End Cob Corner, Only
Side Notched Out on Both   One Side Notched Out
Ends

(Fig. 78.) "A" shows where the end logs and the side wall logs are both notched out to make a perfect corner.

"B" shows how the end is notched out but not the side walls. In this type of construction the logs on the side walls can be spliced with a butt joint or lap joint without detracting from the appearance, while at the same time permitting the use of shorter timbers.

TROUGH TYPE CORNER

This type of corner is not only a job for a skilled mechanic but is also expensive, because of the labor involved and the exactness of measurements between corners. The corner post which must be rabbeted out to receive the offset

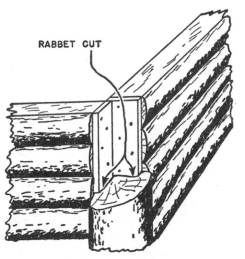

RABBET CUT

Fig. 79   Trough Type Corner

against the right angle 2-inch by 6-inch must fit in snugly and be properly calked. Cutting at a saw mill would be a solution well worth the expense as four or six corners would be the required number needed for a small cabin. Creosoting behind the post and in the corner to prevent nesting of insects of all kinds should be done before placing the corner posts into position. The angle 2-inch by 6-inch should be spiked with galvanized nails. *(Fig. 79.)*

COB CORNERS

In order to have cob corners the log walls should be uniform-faced to the same thickness, such as 8 or 10 inches. Lay the logs in such a way as to make the use of very little chinking and calking necessary between the logs or at the butt ends. The ends should extend about 1 foot and then be trimmed off to not over 6 inches beyond the vertical

Fig. 80   Cob Corners

plumb line at the corner. The ends should be cut close to prevent water from collecting on the flat upper surface of the logs and doing more harm than good. The ends of the logs should be creosoted and oiled several times to prevent shakes from checking the ends as soon as they have been cut. If a saw mill is close by, the small cost involved in having the logs surfaced would compensate for the backbreaking job of doing the work yourself. *(Fig. 80.)*

MORTISE BUTT JOINT

This type of corner applies to cob corner construction and requires quite a little carpentry skill. The logs are left long and cut to a corner line later on. There is bound to be

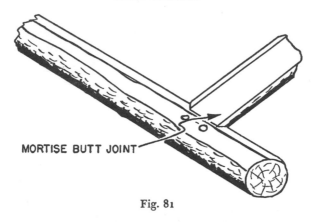

Fig. 81

shrinkage of the logs and if all logs shrink the same amount, the joints will remain intact and require hardly any chinking. The spiking of the corner is done by toe-nailing the spike into the mortised log. *(Fig. 81.)*

CUPPING METHOD

This style of wall construction is not only hard to make, but it takes a mechanic with a fair amount of ability to make a neat job. One advantage is that the shedding of water will

Fig. 82   Cupping Method

be proper since no water can back up into the seams. The calking will last if properly installed. When fitting one log over the other the fit must be good, with a solid footing on the under log. A round curved adze is used to hollow out the groove and notch out for the entire log that it crosses. The logs in this particular instance must be fairly even in diameter to make a neat appearance. *(Fig. 82.)*

NOTCH CORNER

This type of corner is the most common since it is easy to construct. A rounded notch is cut in each log to a depth of half the diameter of the log and rounded so that it fits the log that lays at right angles to it. The notch should fit

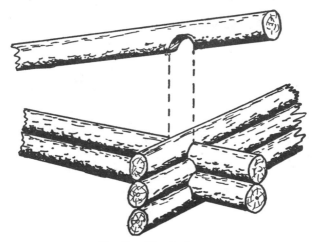

Fig. 83 Notch Corner

fairly close to avoid too much chinking and calking at the corners as this would be unsightly. The extension of an overlapping end is optional, depending upon whether it is to fit a short, close-cut end, or a protruding end to be used for a rail. In the fitting of the logs, the distance between them is important. Correctly spaced and fitted logs will lay firmly on each other, have a good appearance, and will not sag. It is not necessary that they touch at all points but they should rest on each other about every 4 feet. The method of having logs rest only on the notched corners is poor, as the closing and slamming of the doors causes a movement that will affect the chinking, and the wall will be unstable. *(Fig. 83.)*

SADDLE AND NOTCH CORNER

The method of saddle and notch is used to prevent water from seeping into the crevices between the logs and to shed any that might seep through from a driving rain. This cor-

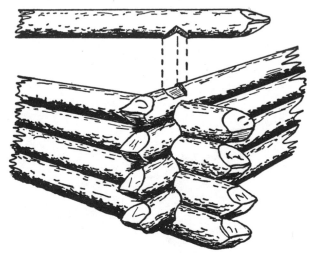

Fig. 84   Saddle and Notch Corner

ner is more difficult to construct than the regular notch, but woodsmen seem to be of the opinion that it is worth the extra work. The ends can be left with a chopped end to give it real pioneer appearance, which many people prefer. If a butt end is desired, it can be cut to suit later. *(Fig. 84.)*

This method of building corners requires a little skill in manipulating the axe, saw and chisel. The logs should be approximately 7 inches in diameter and fairly straight. Section A-A shows the way the end logs are cut. The side and end logs are not interchangeable for either side or end. The

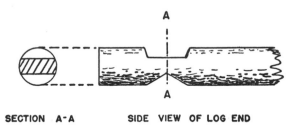

SECTION A-A   SIDE VIEW OF LOG END

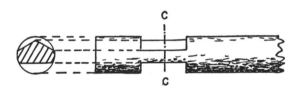

SECTION C-C   SIDE VIEW OF LONGITUDINAL LOGS

Fig. 85   Saddle and Notch

C-C cross-section of the longitudinal logs are cut the same way for both ends if the log reaches the entire length. This type of corner-building method is a modern rather than a pioneer type. *(Fig. 85.)*

The illustration *(fig. 86)* shows how the saddle and notch of the more modern type will come together at the roof line and corner. To make the corner neat and yet watertight, it is better to have the roof line neatly planed with the roof board placed directly on the log wall. Whether the roofing boards run vertically or horizontally on the roof is immaterial, but they should be properly nailed to each log and with at least three nails. The chinking can be carried close to the roofing boards, but it must not be compressed so hard that the roofing boards are loosened and the tightness of the construction impaired.

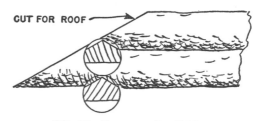

CUT FOR ROOF

Fig. 86   Corner at Roof Line

CORNER DETAIL

Where the cabin is to be built of logs on the sides and stone at the ends there must be a method of keying the end logs into the stone wall so it will be strong and weathertight.

Dovetail the log ends about 4 inches along the entire vertical height of the log as shown. *(Fig. 87.)* This will make a satisfactory keyed-corner. The logs should butt 1½ inches into the wall beyond the shoulder of the dovetail. It is not necessary that all the timbers be dovetailed; every alternate log is sufficient. Care must be taken that the top plate log is dovetailed and properly secured into the wall, as on this particular log much depends. It must be strongly secured and locked to the side walls.

The stone and walls should be approximately 18 inches thick and extend 1 foot beyond the outside surface of the log wall side. The mortar must be imbedded tightly around the dovetail which has previously been heavily painted with creosote. If the stone ends are to be plastered with cement, do not fill the stone joints at the time of laying, but wait until ready for plastering. Filling at this time will help to give a good bond for the plaster coat on the outside. When plastering the outside of a stone wall use more cement in the mixture than lime for this will give a strong durable surface and one less apt to crack, peel, or check. The mixture should be four parts sand, two parts cement, and one part lime. Sand should be screened through a ⅛-inch screen mesh, since unscreened sand does not make a good plaster coat.

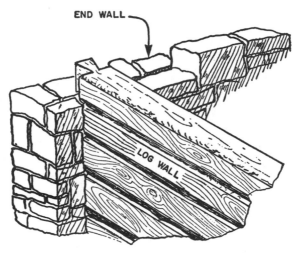

Fig. 87   Corner Detail of Log and Stone

Chapter 10

ROOFS

The roof for a log cabin should conform to the pioneer beauty of thatched, shaked, or other type of antique appearance. The cost of the old types of roofs is a great deal more than if a roll roofing is used. However, roll roofing can be used when the cabin is built, and a more substantial roof put over it later when more time and labor can be utilized. The roof must be built strong, tight and windproof, for a damp house inside takes a long time to dry out before it is ready for occupancy, and musty odors do not disappear over week-end visits. Another item not to be overlooked is to make the roof as fireproof as possible, since fire insurance in the country where fire protection is not available comes very high.

RAFTER AND SECOND FLOOR JOISTS

The weight of a roof, especially one having very little slope and therefore apt to carry a heavy load of snow in the winter, has a tendency to spread the side walls of a cabin apart. Therefore it is essential to have a wall tie such as two threaded rods with a turnbuckle in the center. This is placed through the wall on both sides and threaded with a nut, using a large washer on the outside. When a second floor joist is used, there is no necessity to use wall ties for the joists are keyed into the beam to prevent spreading. A 1-inch by 8-inch ridge board is used to keep the ridge straight and allow nailing from both sides. Short boards are placed between the rafters, driving nails into the top logs so the chinking, which is then filled to the level of the roof line, will not move. *(Fig. 88.)*

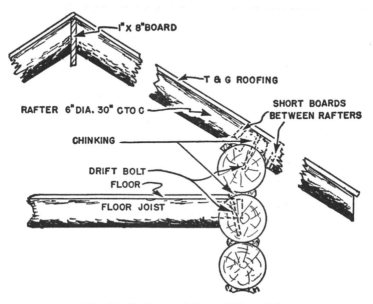

Fig. 88   Rafter and Second Floor Joist

ROOF BRACING

(Fig. 89.) This shows a type of bracing using the "A" tie beams as a supporting member for support of an upper floor. The beams "A" are laid on the beam "B" as shown in the illustration.

(Fig. 90.) A long roof rafter is needed to span the distance from the wall to the ridge near the center of the rafter span so that it can carry the weight of the roof. In this illustration a beam is shown with a cross tie "G" which is dovetailed into beam "H" which rests on the posts. This type of bracing prevents the side walls from spreading if properly tied together.

END VIEW

Fig. 89   Roof Beam

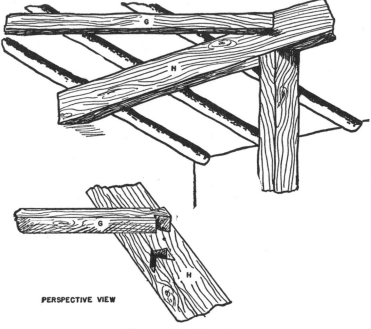

PERSPECTIVE VIEW

Fig. 90   Roof Bracing

THATCHED ROOF

To give a cabin a thatched roof appearance it must have a special built-out roof edge. This type of roof eliminates a cornice of any kind and is made of 1-inch by 2-inch strip

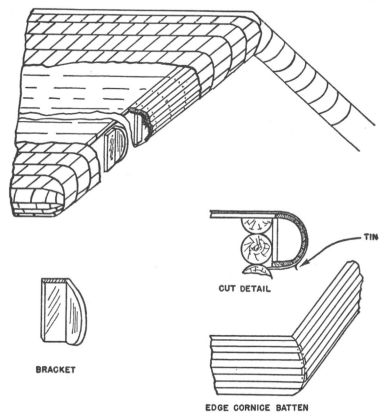

CUT DETAIL

TIN

BRACKET

EDGE CORNICE BATTEN

Fig. 91   Imitation Thatch Roof

battens nailed on brackets. The brackets, made of 1-inch boards, are placed every 10 inches. The outside corners are nailed against each other as shown in the drawing. The shingles are then curved around at the bottom and sides. A galvanized strip of tin is nailed under the edge of the row at the bottom to shed the water away from the side wall. *(Fig. 91.)*

RIDGE BOARD

The ridge of a thatch or shake roof can be finished up with shingles laid as shown. *(Figs. 92, 93, 94.)* If there is a chimney that protrudes at the ridge line start the shingles from each end, but if there is no chimney on the ridge start from one end and finish up at the other, or start from both ends, finishing in the middle, the final shingle to be placed so the grain is vertical with the horizontal line of the roof. In starting use a double shingle to give it the same pitch on the roof level. The width of the ridge shingles should be dressed so they all keep a straight line across the roof. At the ridge top, to prevent the roof from leaking, the shingles should be bevel-planed to insure a tight fit, alternating the joints so that one will not come directly over the other. "A" and "B" are alternating ridge joints, and "C" is a joint in the center.

CURVED SHINGLE LINE

An irregular curved line for shingles gives the roof a shake roof appearance. *(Fig. 95.)* This requires a great deal of work because the bottom edge of the shingles has to be cut to various curved lines. A tarred felt paper should be installed over clapboards or tongue and grooved roofing boards. When starting the first row of shingles at the bottom of the roof, double that row and allow the shingles to protrude 3 inches over the edge of the roofing strip. They can be cut off later. Then start the next shingle anywhere from 3 inches to 8 inches to the weather depending on the curve wanted. The best method of doing this is to make a straight edge with irregular curves on it and place this on the roof line, cutting the shingles to fit the curves. Use a coping saw but hold the

Fig. 92 Six-Inch Ridge Board

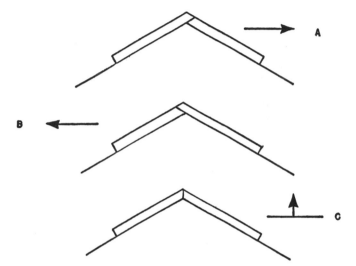

Fig. 93 Ridge Construction

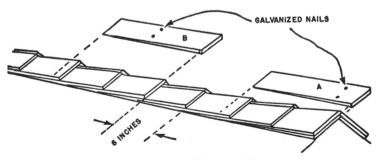

Fig. 94 Cedar Shingle Ridge

shingles tightly between two boards otherwise they will split when sawing. Where a heavier thickness of shingles is desired, lay a shingle underneath the regular row horizontally and

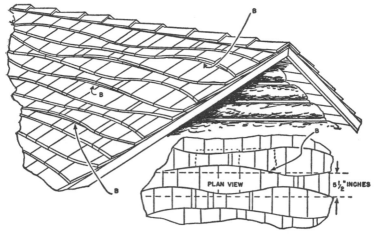

Fig. 95   Curved Row Shingle Roof

feather it out on top (which means to thin the edge) so it will become smooth with the roof again, as shown in illustration "B."

IMITATION SHAKE ROOF

This type of roof can be laid with offset shingle rows to give a shake roof effect. It will look very fitting for a log cabin. Regular commercial cedar shingles (drag faced), are recommended, not over 8 inches in width. The offset can be any distance from ¼ inch to 3 inches. Be careful that the distance between the offset and the next course of shingles does not extend more than half the length of the shingles, or the water shed from the roof will seep behind the under shingle between the top shingle cracks. It is best to leave about ⅛ inch

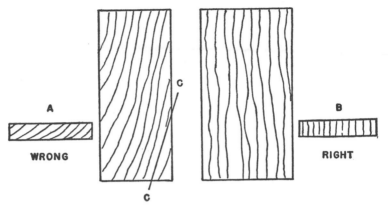

A   C   C   B

WRONG   RIGHT

Fig. 96   Cutting of Wooden Shingles

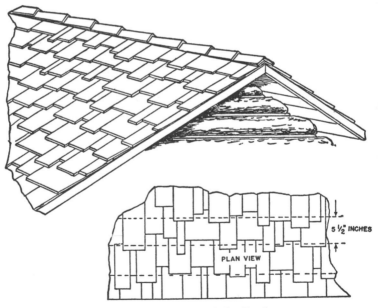

5 ½" INCHES

PLAN VIEW

Fig. 97   Imitation Shake Roof

between each shingle for expansion due to wet weather. These shingles should be nailed with galvanized nails. The roofing boards should be tongue and grooved or shiplap boards, with a tarpaper felt placed over them. Place the height of the shingle rows not more than 5½ inches for a happy medium to make the roof waterproof. Diagonal-grained shingles could be used for filler or first row starters to be covered up. Shingle "A" *(fig. 96)* is apt to crack or break at line "c-c" and cause leakage. "B" is a good shingle and would last indefinitely. Painting or creosoting will help to preserve wooden shingles.

Chapter 11

FLOORS

FLOOR CONSTRUCTION OFF THE GROUND

When it becomes necessary to build a floor on posts, pillars, etc., some sturdy type of beam is important. In the type of construction shown *(fig. 98),* the main carrying beam has the floor joists notched into them with a tenon 4 inches by 6 inches, and

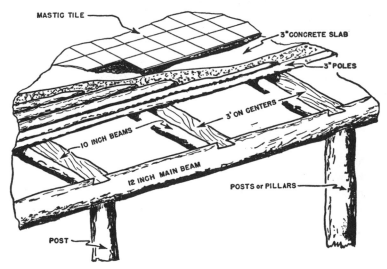

Fig. 98 Floor Construction off Ground

4 inches deep. On top of the floor joists are 3-inch to 4-inch poles laid close together, stripped of the bark and creosoted. The concrete is then laid on top approximately 3 inches thick, and a mastic tile floor laid on top of it to keep it sanitary. If no

mastic tile is used, the concrete floor can be painted with a good heavy concrete paint and carpets used for warmth.

STRENGTHENING MAIN FLOOR BEAMS OF CABIN ON STILTS

If a log cabin is built on stilts or over a bluff or lake a very important item may be overlooked by the inexperienced builder. The main beam on which the cabin floor joists rest

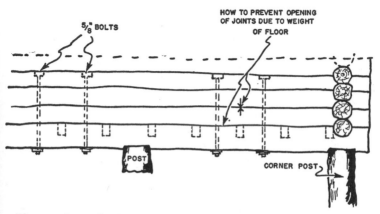

Fig. 99   Strengthening Main Floor Beams of Log Cabin on Posts

must be strengthened if the span is 10 feet or more between the supporting posts. This strengthening is done after the first three or four side wall logs are set in place. Seven-eighths-inch holes are drilled through the three wall logs and the beam. A long bolt is then dropped in place with the nut on the bottom so it can be tightened up at any time. *(Fig. 99.)*

FLOOR BEAM CONSTRUCTION

In the floor beam construction of a cabin, whether for the first or second floors, the joists are mortised into the beam or wall in the manner shown. If the first floor beam is to be placed on pillars it should be strong enough to carry the weight of the floor. The floor joists should not be spaced any farther apart than 16 inches if ⅞-inch floor boards are to be used, or 3 feet apart for 2-inch plank flooring. The planking should be dressed on all four sides and thoroughly dry when installed,

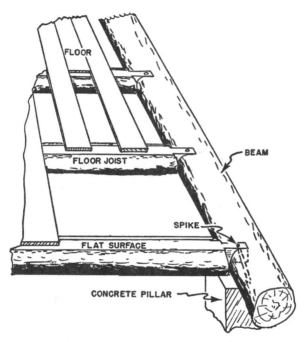

Fig. 100   Floor Beam Construction

being spiked with two nails in each joist. The mortise should have an end tenon 3 x 8 inches with one spike fastening it to the beam. Drill a hole in the tenon and the beam with a gimlet drill, making the hole slightly smaller than the diameter of the spike. (*Fig. 100.*)

CONCRETE FLOOR

A concrete floor is most economical for a cabin floor when no basement is desired. Mice are not able to penetrate the floor although they may bore their homes underneath with entrance from outside the cabin. The drawing (*fig. 101*) shows at "A" the finished floor of 1-inch concrete, at "B" **2 inches of**

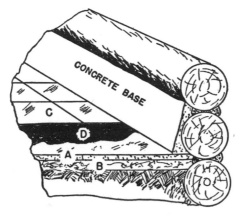

Fig. 101   Concrete Floor

grouting, at "C" the mastic tile, and at "D" the cement that holds the mastic tile to the concrete. The mastic tile is not affected by water, but will become soft if gasoline and kerosene are spilled on it. A concrete base is cemented against the log to make a neat corner.

Chapter 12

WINDOWS AND DOORS

A cabin with cheery windows large enough to admit a substantial amount of air to keep dampness out and to circulate through the rooms is necessary for enjoyable cabin life. Do not build small windows such as the porthole type unless you intend to have plenty of them. But do not make them too large unless you have provisions to carry the load weight over them. Many large plate glass windows have been added to cabins of the sunporch variety, but the drying of the wood shrinks the wall, and if weight is pressed on the glass itself you are apt to have a broken window. A good strong inner frame will do much to keep the weight from the glass top and also prevent the log sides from twisting if the logs are properly spiked to it. The doors, like the windows, should have strong frames. A 3' x 7' door for the main entrance for admittance of a piano or other large furniture is desirable, but the other doors throughout the house can be the average 2'8" x 6'8" style. Make the door to conform with the pioneer atmosphere for harmony.

HARDWARE

The hardware for cabin doors and windows is similar to that on any house. The logs can be fastened with trunnels or large spikes, or ⅝-inch iron rods set with a set tool. When logs are to be spiked together, drill a hole through the log to help the spike along. When driving a spike into hard wood, drill a hole ¹⁄₃₂-inch larger than the spike through the first log, where it is to be placed, while the log into which it is fastened should have the hole $\frac{1}{32}$-inch smaller than the spike or rod. The window spring bolt is fastened into a hole snugly so it will not move around. If it does, glue a few turns of a newspaper around it, and then drive it in from the sliding surface of the window.

WALL AND WINDOW DETAIL FOR HALF WALL HEIGHT CABIN

(*Fig. 102.*) In this illustration is shown a view of a side wall ending on the window sill line when the continuation of the logs for a side wall is desired. It is not necessary to wait to im-

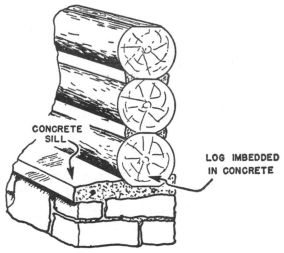

CONCRETE SILL

LOG IMBEDDED IN CONCRETE

Fig. 102   Wall Detail

bed the first log in the cement as shown. This can be done when the cabin is ready for the chinking. Supports are placed between the log and wall approximately every 4 feet, and the butt end of the log. These supports should be made of stone chips and mason cement which is a mixture of 3 parts sand, 1 part lime, and 1 part Portland cement. This makes a strong and workable mortar.

(Fig. 103.) This illustration shows a cut view of a window, with concrete sill, placed on a stone wall. Windows should be placed on the same sill height by resting them on stone chip

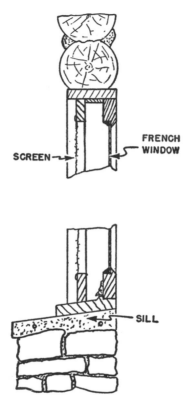

SCREEN

FRENCH WINDOW

SILL

Fig. 103   Window Detail

supports, bracing them from the ground with stakes for a hold-fast. The concrete sill can be cemented underneath the window at the same time the rest of the sill is installed. The sill should have a reinforcing of wire or small ¼-inch pickled rods to prevent cracking. Screens should be placed outside the windows whether they are double hung or French style windows. Most cabins have French inswinging windows so when hot weather arrives the window can be tied back and the full daylight opening of the window utilized for air.

DUTCH DOOR

This type of door in two sections is used when it is desirable to have only half of it closed at a time. It has a watershed over it. The bottom section has a small shelf with a stop which fits

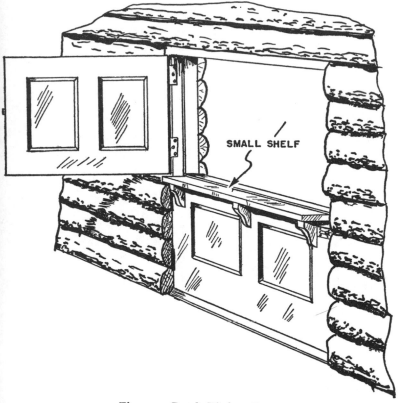

SMALL SHELF

Fig. 104   Dutch Kitchen Door

tightly against the upper door section. There are two hinges on each upper and lower section and a latch on both sections so they may be locked from the inside. A screen door may be set outside the Dutch door so that half of it can be kept open, but it is more customary to use this type of door as entrance from a screened porch. *(Fig. 104.)*

WINTER SHUTTERS

When closing up for the winter it is advisable to cover the windows with shutters which are fastened from the inside. A small moon or other design can be placed in the shutter to

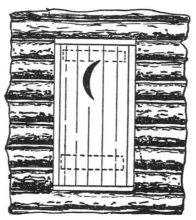

Fig. 105   Winter Shutters

give it a ventilating hole. Covering the windows on the outside will help to save glass and be a protection against petty thievery. *(Fig. 105.)*

FRENCH WINDOW DETAIL

(Fig. 106.) "A" shows the plan view of a French window with a rabbeted jamb against the 2- x 8-inch inner jamb. This is the most popular log cabin type of window.

"B" shows the bottom sill fit snugly between the side jambs and as tightly as possible down on the log. The top of the sill is beveled to give it a slope to shed water and rabbeted on the inside to receive the French window.

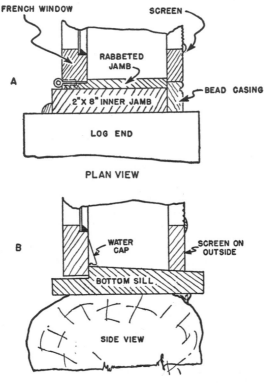

Fig. 106   French Window Detail

OUTSIDE CASINGS

This method of casing up a door or window is used to give the log cabin a cottage effect, and it will give a full size casing on the outside to receive screens or storm sash. The ends of the logs that butt against the window or door jamb are chamfered with a straight bevel or gentle curve to the casing edge, whichever suits the individual's taste. The casing is 4 inches wide and 1⅛ inches thick. The back of the casings should be painted and dried before they are nailed in place.

Fig. 107   Casings on Outside of Door and Window

A calking compound, which looks like soft putty should be run under the casing before the casing is set. The drip caps on the top of doors and windows are covered with a copper flashing and nailed every inch on the log side. *(Fig. 107.)*

WINDOW JAMB DETAIL

This illustration *(fig. 108)* shows how window spring bolts are installed in the upper sash at about the center of the height of a window light. The parting bead is set in a groove

⅜" deep and nailed. The window side jamb is nailed to the
2 x 8 blind jamb that holds the logs in place.

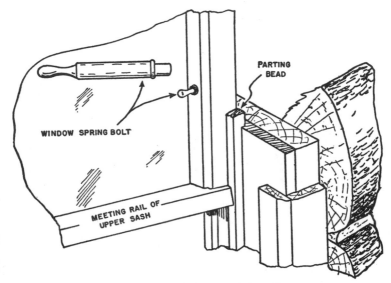

Fig. 108   Window Jamb Detail

WINDOW SPRING BOLT

Spring bolts are inexpensive and are placed on each side
near the middle of the upper and lower sash, forcing them
into a hole drilled so they fit snugly. The holes should be
drilled half way from the inside glass surface and the inside
of the sash surface. The bolts are then driven in from the
outside of the sash. You can place these in the sash as soon
as they are fitted.

For locking the upper window in place, raise the window
up to its full height and strike the bolts on each side so they
will mark the jamb. Now lower the sash and drill a hole
about ½ inch deep in each jamb where the mark was made.
Various locking heights can be given the window by drill-

ing corresponding holes on each side for both the upper and lower sashes. The lower sash should have the holes drilled for the bottom locking position. There is no need of a window lock at the meeting rail if window spring bolts are used.

DETAIL OF WINDOW BOLT

This plan view *(fig. 109)* shows how a window jamb and window spring bolts are placed into the sash and window jamb. The illustration is for a double sliding window with a spring bolt lock. If double hung windows are used a sash weight pocket must be built in the window frame and the logs cut to fit. This is not customary unless an expensive type of cabin is built.

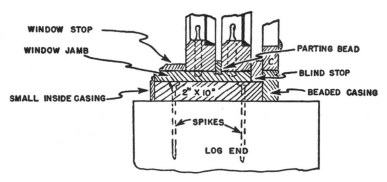

Fig. 109   Detail of Window Bolt Plan View

Chapter 13

PORCH AND GARAGE

HILLSIDE CABIN

A cabin placed on a hillside, even though far from any lake or stream, can be made just as comfortable as any other. In the cabin illustrated in *fig. 110* the front entrance is toward the roadway and a side stairway is built into the slope of the ground leading to the rear of the house where there is a driveway to a two-car garage.

Fig. 110   Porch over Garage

This cabin of generous dimensions includes a large fireplace and a screened-in porch over the garage. The basement with its double windows is light and roomy and provides space that can be used for dancing, lounging, or storage. An

inside door provides entry between the garage and the basement, with an inside stairway extending from the basement
to the first floor. Puddles of water caused by rainy weather,
or from washing the car, are prevented by having both the
driveway and the garage floor slope gently away from the house.
Trees and shrubbery can be planted around the house for
decorative purposes, and, if properly insulated, this type of
cabin could be used for an all-year-round house. A heating
plant and a compressed-air water supply system may be installed. A pump for drinking water is essential and should
be on or near the property.

The dormer slab logs are placed vertically to save timber
and the foundation is made of quarry rock or cobblestones.
When building a foundation of cobblestones it is advisable
to build it 2 feet thick and place plenty of wall ties in its
construction to avoid cracking. If a cobblestone surface foundation is backed with reinforced concrete it is not necessary
to build it heavier than 18 inches thick.

A concrete floor with a ⅛-inch mastic tile covering is suitable for the basement floor.

The garage doors which swing outward to allow more
space for the cars, have small 18-inch by 18-inch glass windows.

WEEK-END LOG CABIN

A low bungalow type log cabin with a water shed for an
automobile near the door entrance is useful. This type of
cabin is built for rainy weather as well as fair weather. A
fireplace at one end and windows on three sides give warmth
and light. Light also enters through a window in the entrance
door on the shed side. The water shed should be closed at one
end as a means of keeping the car dry. No repairs which in-
volve the use of gasoline should be attempted on the car
while it is under the shelter, because of fire hazards. The

cabin proper is 20 feet by 20 feet, and can have a large living room with folding bunks, one bedroom, and a cooking corner which can be either enclosed or open. A ceiling can be installed over each room or the living room left open to give it a studio effect. *(Fig. 111.)*

Fig. 111   Week-end Cabin with Car Shelter

AN OVERHANGING PORCH

A cellar built in the side of a hill should always have stone walls. The reason for this is to keep the basement dry as well as long-lasting. Logs will not last long in the ground where water seepage comes in contact with them continually making them a water stop. This cabin is built on a stone foundation and the end logs protrude beyond the foundation to make an overhanging porch. The three protruding logs are anchored in the length of the entire side wall to prevent sagging. Light in the basement is provided by a small window and by a Dutch door which is also an exit. A half log stool is used for a seat under the porch. If the basement is to be used for living quarters rather than storage, a larger window should be used. *(Fig. 112.)*

Fig. 112   An Overhanging Porch

Chapter 14

INTERIOR AND EXTERIOR OF CABIN

The appearance of the interior of the cabin depends on individual taste. Some would keep the surroundings antique and odd, others would decorate with Indian blankets and objects. Still other individuals would use the old wagon wheel and prairie atmosphere, while some would use the gay nineties style.

Try making your own furniture, which not only looks attractive but gives you a certain feeling of pride for having made it yourself.

The exterior of the cabin can be finished off later when time will allow, but is a harder job and may dislodge or crack some of the chinking if too much pounding is done. There are many surfaces described in this book.

It is necessary to keep a constant lookout for insects that may destroy the wood surface. A thorough inspection each spring with creosoting or painting will give longer life to the cabin.

PULLMAN BUNKS

Where space is at a premium this type of sleeping quarters is satisfactory when one family can occupy the same room. The fireplace could be placed at any side of the room and may be simply for decorative purposes; or better yet, its cheery heat can remove chill and dampness from the air. The closet between the bunks provides a storage space. The bunks should be approximately 4 feet inside and 8 feet long. The bottom of the first tier of the bunk should have a clearance of 10 inches under which to slide a grip, and the top tier should not be any higher than is easily accessible with the aid of a small ladder. Maximum utilization of the space in a small cabin can be obtained with this type of built-in sleeping quarters. *(Fig. 113.)*

Fig. 113   Pullman Bunks

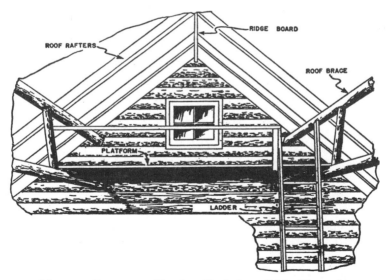

Fig. 114   Emergency Sleeping Nook in a Cabin Mezzanine

CABIN NOOK OR MEZZANINE

In a large cabin with a studio room extending to the roof, it may be necessary to run roof braces the length of the room, along the mid-line of the rafters, as shown. *(Fig. 114.)* These roof braces may be used to support a temporary mezzanine or nook. To make an emergency sleeping nook, a layer of 2-inch planking is placed across the span, resting on the lower timber braces, and a rail and ladder are used to prevent falling off and for gaining admittance to the nook. The entire platform and ladder can be removed in a short time by one man and stored somewhere else until needed again.

HAGGLE SURFACE

Haggle gouging of timbers gives a surface an antique effect but it is difficult and requires skilled handling of a rounded adze or a large round gouge. For the proper effect, only square logs should be used, and only the outside surface is haggled. It must be remembered that a surface with less knots and checks will give a better appearance. There are two methods: one is to cut along the grain of the logs, and the other crosswise of the logs. For this type of work only a skilled manipulator of the adze can do a neat job. *(Fig. 115.)*

CEILING UP INSIDE OF CABIN

Whether the ceiling boards are placed horizontally or vertically against the side walls is immaterial. Fastening the ceiling directly to the logs is inexpensive but a true line of surfacing the logs is necessary and the job of chopping is quite difficult to one not having any experience. An adze can be used to great advantage. If the ceiling boards are placed horizontally there is no method of keeping mice out. However, if the ceiling boards are placed vertically, whether on a furring strip or not, all open crevices can be filled with broken glass packed in as tightly as possible. Place bottles in the space and

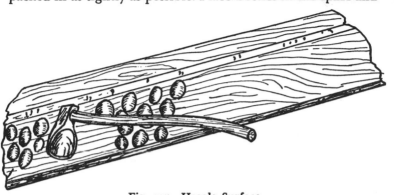

Fig. 115   Haggle Surface

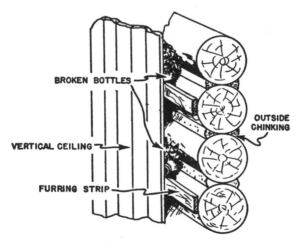

Fig. 116

break them up with a steel rod, or use broken glass and pack full. Window glass is not suitable; bottle or irregular shapes are preferred. Mice will stay clear of this space to avoid cutting their feet. (*Fig. 116.*)

FURRING STRIPS FOR PLASTERING

In this illustration *(fig. 117)* the logs have been sized to 8 inches and surfaced on three sides, the finished width being

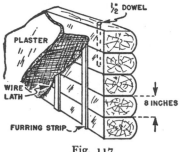

12 inches. They are creosoted on the three surface sides and stacked on top of each other and may have any type of corner desired. The furring strips are placed 16 inches from the center of one to the center of the other. The wire lath is then placed over them and plastered. If there is any settling or shrink-

Fig. 117

age of the logs, it is less apt to be taken up by the cracking of the plaster, and the small air space between the plaster and log acts as an insulator. The logs are held together by wooden dowels 1½ inches in diameter.

PLASTERING INSIDE

Placing wire lath inside against the flat surface of logs is done though it is not good practice. Shifting or settling of the cabin by shrinkage will cause cracks in the plaster which

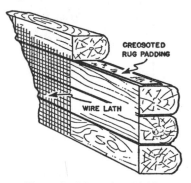

Fig. 118   Plastering Inside

become a constant repair job. For a calking joint, creosoted rug padding can be used as well as oakum without sacrificing attractiveness. *(Fig. 118.)*

PLANED GOUGE SURFACE

A gouged surface can be made with a plane known as a scrub plane which has a 1-inch iron with a round cutting surface, beveled behind the cutting edge. A scrub plane can

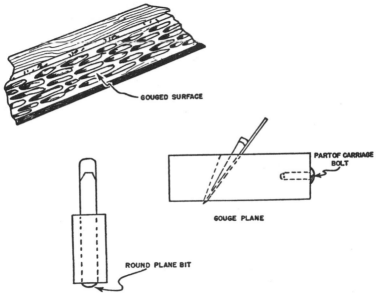

Fig. 119   How to Make Gouge Surface

be purchased, or made from a small narrow wagon spring, merely straightening it out and putting a cutting edge on the face. A wedge holds the plane iron in place. A carriage bolt with a large head is inserted into the back of the plane and is struck with a hammer to remove the iron. Long or short gouging cuts can be made with this plane but it is a hard surface for an inexperienced man to make. A gouging chisel is helpful to start and finish the groove. *(Fig. 119.)*

BURNING HAGGLE SURFACE

When burning in a haggle surface use six or seven iron rods bent in a small circle and heat them all in the same fire. Use a pair of heavy leather gloves to handle the irons

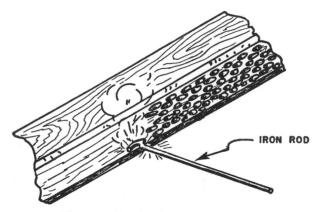

— IRON ROD

Fig. 120   Burning in a Haggle Surface

as they may be hot. After the surface is burnt in, remove all charcoal with a steel brush, wash with turpentine, and soak with stained creosote. After it has dried, varnish the surface with spar or plastic varnish. *(Fig. 120.)*

STAIRS TO UPPER FLOOR

When stairs are needed for a cabin, a pair of dressed logs are placed to form the stair slope which you desire. The total height from the top of the finished first floor to the top of the finished second floor is divided by the height of the step riser to find the number of steps needed. The riser height is the distance from the top of one stair tread to the top of the next stair tread. If the stairs are steep the width of a stair tread should not be less than an 8-inch dressed plank, but should there be less slope it may be preferable to have a dressed 10-inch plank as a tread. It must be remembered that a step height can range from 7½ to 9 inches in an ordinary home. The first step can then be cut in, keeping all the steps the same height. When nailing the treads on the log the edge should protrude over the vertical cut approximately 1 inch. A stick which has the divided height of the risers marked on it can be placed on the floor as a vertical gauge for marking off each step. *(Fig. 121.)*

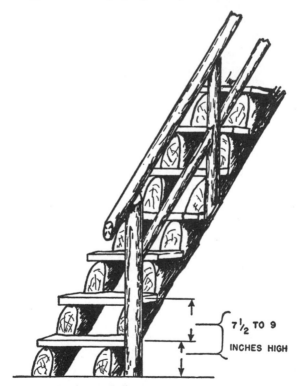

Fig. 121 Stairs to Upper Floor

Chapter 15

FIREPLACES

BUILDING A FIREPLACE

Planning location, size and general character of a fireplace before the cabin is built is very important. Many factors are involved. It may be an old fashioned fireplace as used in the pioneer days with a damper which can be operated from the face side and a fireplace crane to swing the cooking kettles over the fire. The fireplace could be built of hard burnt brick or field stones. If built of field stones it should be backed up with firebrick, as intense heat causes field stones to check and in time they will crumble.

Another factor involved is the chimney. It is a definite feature of the exterior architecture. In some cases its location in the floor plan is determined by the desirability of enclosing several chimney flues in the same stack enclosure, including one for a stove or a heating plant in the basement.

In selecting the chimney location, both practicability and utility are important factors. Consideration of proportions, such as comparing the size of the fireplace to the size of the room as a whole, the way in which it will be used, and the decorative scheme must all be contemplated. It becomes necessary for the designer of a home to visualize to what extent the users of his fireplace will enjoy its comforts for relaxation and cooking. Many a home in pioneer days was a long narrow building with one fireplace in the center, or one on each end, upon which the various rooms depended for heating facilities. The most convenient space is likely to be found at the side or end of a room. A fireplace set in the end of a room is very likely to be preferable on grounds of seclusion. A side position may avoid the crowding of furniture.

With the present day simplification of home life, it is not surprising to find more interest in the smaller fireplaces. Rustic and early colonial period types are characteristic of log cabin fireplaces, but any period of design can be built without being bound by its traditions.

The fireplace may extend wholly into the room, or stand flush with the wall, or project for a part of its depth away from the wall. The present day trend seems to be the flush type, though the projection type affords space for fuel containers and fire tools, and it also helps to emphasize the fireplace. For best results the fireplace should be built against an outer wall, with a chimney solely for use with it.

The old tenement fireplace consisting of a hole in the wall, with little or no flue, and having its front wall made of various colored tiles, is hardly a sufficient fireplace for any cabin. The designs of Georgian and Colonial periods are found in early American homes. They had the advantage of being produced in a time in which simple technique ruled.

In many log cabins such as those in which our ancestors were born during the seventeenth and eighteenth centuries, a single fireplace served all purposes. It was built of native material, usually of rough masonry coordinated with rough-hewn timbers. It had a swinging crane on which the pots and kettles could be hung and removed from the fire without lifting them off the crane.

Preference seems to be toward the fireplace of rugged stone masonry, employing field stones or choice specimens picked up from distant places, hewn and coordinated into a desirable design to suit the owner.

The question of size of fireplace must be taken into consideration, as a large size fireplace with a small flue may smoke excessively. It is not advisable to build a fireplace that will give more heat than is desired, as the room may be uncomfortably warm; a 30-inch fireplace is large enough for an average room of 15 x 15 feet.

The damper throat should be made so as to take care of smoke and gases. If the supply of air is sufficient for proper combustion, and the flue opening large enough to allow the gases to escape, the fireplace will not smoke. It takes air for draft and oxygen for combustion to keep a fire burning to its full capacity. Making a room airtight will not allow sufficient air for proper combustion in a fireplace, and also there is apt to be a downdraft which will prevent maintaining a fire on the hearth. A small opening from the cellar or an outside ventilating device is desirable.

FLUE LINING SIZES

Flue linings come in 2-foot lengths and have round corners approximately ⅝ inch in radius. The thickness of the material is about ¾ inch.

The following sizes are manufactured, the measurements being the outside dimensions:

Standard Size of Flue Lining, Outside	Greatest Area of Fireplace Opening
8½" x 13"	Approx. 2'0" x 3'0"
8½" x 18"	" 2'8" x 3'0"
12" x 16"	" 3'0" x 3'7"
13" x 13"	" 3'0" x 3'1"
14" x 16"	" 3'2" x 4'0"
16" x 16"	" 3'9" x 4'0"
16" x 20"	" 4'2" x 4'6"
18" x 18"	" 4'2" x 4'6"

For larger size fireplace openings use two flue linings in place of one.

The dampers in the upper smoke chamber must not have

an opening smaller in area than the area of the inside of the flue in each particular fireplace dimension.

HEATSAVER

In this illustration (*fig. 122*) the heatsaver is shown enclosed in a brick wall. If placed against an inner partition the wall must have a row of bricks or other fireproofing material to safeguard the wall against fire.

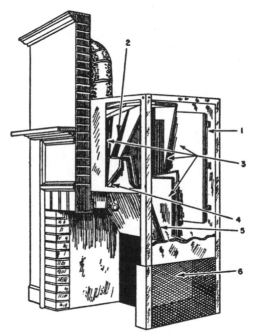

Fig. 122   Section Shows Inside Construction of Heatsaver

1—Shows large warm air chamber.

2—Warm air duct through smoke chamber that equalizes the heat.

3—Baffle sheets keep outer shell cool and increase delivery of heat through ducts.

4—Donley poker control damper.

5—Quarter-inch steel plate used for smoke shelf and back of fire chamber.

6—Cold air inlet screened to prevent entrance of rodents.

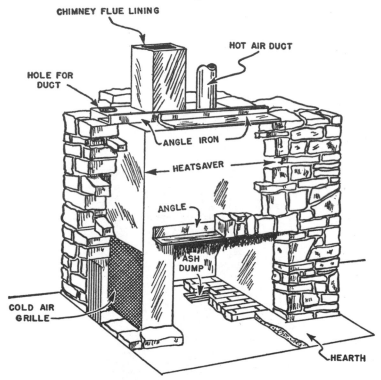

Fig. 123 Heatsaver Encased in Quarry Stone

All fireplaces should have a screen to prevent sparks from reaching rugs or upholstered furniture, especially when the fireplace is in use without constant watching.

This illustration (*fig. 123*) shows a heatsaver encased in quarry stone. By using this type of fireplace, more heat is dispensed through heating of the back and side plates which are on one side of the vent ducts. The cold air let in at one side near the bottom flows up in contact with the heated sides of the firebox and, becoming heated, it rises rapidly through the air ducts and flows out into the room elsewhere. This warm air is added to the regular heat that is given off from the opening in the fireplace and will warm a room sooner and better than the regular type of fireplace.

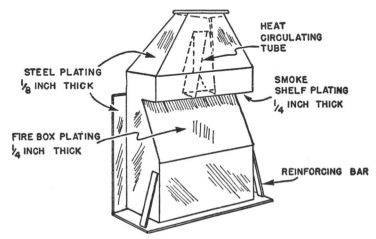

Fig. 124   Back View of Heatsaver

If an ash dump is placed in the fireplace floor, the hot ashes should not be allowed to come in contact with wood or any part of the log cabin structure. Should the log cabin have a cellar, an enclosed stone or brick ash pit can be made under the fireplace. The ashes can then be dumped from the floor above, and then taken out through the ashpit door.

This illustration (*fig. 124*) shows the back view of the heatsaver fireplace. This is a manufactured fireplace that will conserve a greater amount of heat than a fireplace made in the regular manner. The heat that penetrates the firebox plate is dispensed from a side vent on the upper side of the fireplace as in the old type of pot-bellied stove. In the regular type of fireplace most of this heat would pass up the flue.

One of the details that must not be overlooked in building a fireplace is the size of the opening. The fireplace opening should not exceed ten times the area of the flue. Thus, if a flue measures 10 inches by 10 inches inside, the fireplace opening

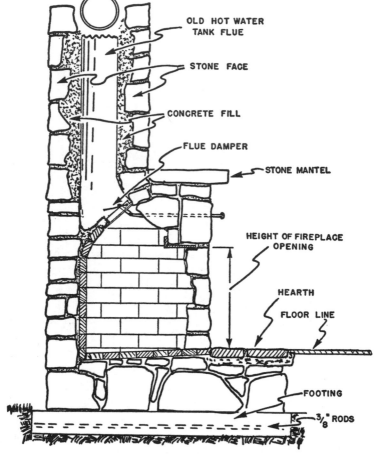

OLD HOT WATER
TANK FLUE

STONE FACE

CONCRETE FILL

FLUE DAMPER

STONE MANTEL

HEIGHT OF FIREPLACE
OPENING

HEARTH

FLOOR LINE

FOOTING

3/8" RODS

Fig. 125   Fireplace Construction

should be less than 1,000 square inches in area, such as would be obtained with a 33-inch by 30-inch opening. Fire brick should be used on the fireplace floor, side and back as high as the damper. The damper can be purchased from some hardware dealer and should be provided with a long handle to be operated from the side or front of the fireplace. An old hot-water tank can be used for a concrete inner form and left there if a stone faced chimney is filled around it, but a wire or steel reinforcement must be added to prevent it from cracking. (*Fig. 125.*)

CHIMNEY CAP

A chimney cap can be of any design that is desired, but it must be reinforced with ¼-inch pickled rods to prevent the cap from cracking. A large sewer pipe makes a good flue lining, or flue lining pipe can be used. A chimney can also be made by cutting the top and bottom off an old hot water tank with a torch, then welding or riveting the pieces together. Let the flue, whether it be single, double or triple stacked, protrude a little above the cap. The chimney should be at least 4 feet above the ridge of the cabin to give the fireplace a good draft. (*Fig. 126.*)

Fig. 126   Chimney Cap

FLASHING AROUND CHIMNEY

When fitting flashing around a chimney, place the flashing tins in the mortar joints of the stone. Be sure to place a little mortar on the stone first, putting a little mortar on the tin also, and let the weight of the additional stone hold the

Fig. 127   Flashing around Chimney

tin in place. Perforate the tin along the inner edge with a nail so the burrs will help hold the tin more firmly. The flashing can be made of copper or galvanized iron to make it longer lasting. Lay the roof, and nail the flashing with copper or galvanized nails. Always nail the flashing every inch along the outer edge. Paint freely, or use calking compound between the lap joints to help tighten the joint. (*Fig. 127.*)

WALL TIES

When building a chimney of stone or cobblestone, it is important that wall ties be used to keep the stones together so there will be no cracking when finished. A piece of galvanized tin about 1 inch wide and 12 inches long should be cut out, and a $\frac{1}{4}$-inch hole punched into it on each end, as

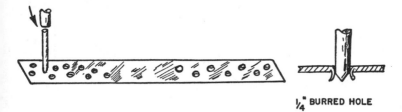

$\frac{1}{4}$" BURRED HOLE

Fig. 128   Making Wall Ties

shown, with a blunt punch. The burred hole is relied on to hold the mortar together. Any salvage tin can be used but galvanized iron is less apt to rust and will last longer. (*Fig. 128.*)

FUNDAMENTAL BUILDING RULES

The building of a fireplace is not a difficult job even to the inexperienced individual if a few fundamental rules are followed. One of the first rules for a substantial fireplace is a good footing, large enough to prevent any settling and reinforced with steel rods to prevent cracking.

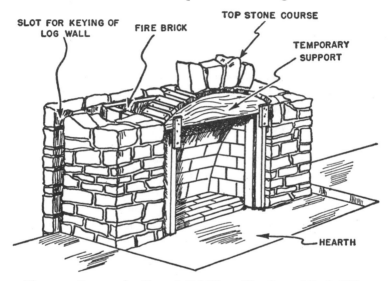

Fig. 129   Support for Top of Old Time Fireplace while Building

The hearth is part of the foundation of the fireplace and should be extended up to the floor level. If the hearth is to be covered with brick, flagging, or marble, the thicknesses of these surfaces should be left below the desired floor level, as shown in *fig. 129*, for the time being. It is best to leave the hearth surface until the entire fireplace and stack are finished.

The inside of the fireplace, where the direct heat from the fire causes very high temperatures, should be covered with firebrick. This is done to prevent the fire from cracking the stone.

If a fireplace has a straight top, two angle irons should be placed heel to heel with long flange surfaces set to carry the stone above the fireplace. When a curved top is desired a temporary support must be built to carry the weight of the stone until it has been completed and dried out. This can be accomplished by cutting two 2 x 10's to the desired curvature and nailing 1-inch x 1½-inch strips of wood between them so that they are separated by about 10 inches. The temporary support is held up by four 2 x 4's, two on each side, and nailed to the upper curved section, which must fit snugly between the sides as shown. To avoid a temporary structure two angle irons could be heated and bent to the shape desired, employing the same method that is used on the straight top.

A few choice stones should be placed over the top of the fireplace, fitting them neatly in place. Be sure you fill the lower joints fully; otherwise you must fill these joints after the temporary supports have been removed.

If the fireplace is placed in such a position that the outside or inside wall ends in it, it is best to provide a slot in the fireplace wall so the ends of the logs can be keyed into this slot to a depth of 6 to 8 inches. This slot is to extend up the entire height of the wall to the roof and should be chinked tightly to prevent leaks of air, or if on the outside to prevent rain or snow from seeping into the cabin.

The shelf or mantel for the fireplace should be of choice flat stones with a neat front edge to exploit the beauty of the fireplace.

LARGE FIREPLACE

A large fireplace at one end of the room with closed-in book cases on each side that fill up the entire end of a room, is a suggestion which is not only practical but economical. This type of fireplace will need a high ceiling, or should be used in a cabin more spacious than a small week-end cabin. The mantel can be made of wood, marble or a 3-inch thick flagging, or if a mould is made, it can be of concrete. The

Fig. 130   Large Fireplace

stones might be cut from a quarry in the neighborhood or cut from large cobblestones. Two large angle irons, ⅜ inch thick, with a 6-inch flange over the opening will be necessary to hold the header stones in place. A certain overlapping bond to each row of stones is desirable with large mortar joints. *(Fig. 130.)*

BRICK COLONIAL FIREPLACE

A hard brick fireplace of the Colonial type is easier to build than one made of stone. This particular fireplace, ex-

tending about 3 feet into the room, is placed against an
interior wall, and has an oven on the left side. The mantel
and faceboard are nailed to keyed wooden blocks, which have
been set into the brickwork for that purpose. A fireplace
looks bare unless it has its just supplies. *(Fig. 131.)*

Fig. 131   Brick Colonial Fireplace

EARLY AMERICAN STONE FIREPLACE

This quarry stone fireplace *(fig. 132)* is characteristic of the
early American type. Native stone was used in this fireplace
and the end of the log cabin was keyed into its structure.
The broad mantel and faceboard provide sufficient room for
a flintlock rifle and powder horn. The old saying "keep your
powder dry and ready at all times" had a meaning to all
pioneers in those log cabin days. The large crane which
could be swung over the fire had several notches on the

top surface to hold the pots apart so they would not slide off
or bump into each other.

Fig. 132   Early American Stone Fireplace

STACKING WOOD

Where trees are felled for firewood, a place for stacking and
drying in preparation for winter use is an important matter.
Green wood cannot be readily burned and needs a certain
amount of drying and seasoning. To stack the wood in neat
piles, a post can be imbedded into the ground and a brace
placed into the ground against the post. The wood should be
stacked as high as it can conveniently be reached. Sometimes
a stack can be placed around the yard as a fence or windbreak. The wood should be covered in winter as a protection
against snow. *(Fig. 133.)*

BUILDING A FIRE IN A FIREPLACE

In building an open fire the best woods to use are hickory, apple, cherry and oak. Make a cradle of kindling on the andirons by laying some pieces lengthwise and others across, and on this lay two logs separated slightly. Arrange more kindling

Fig. 133   Drying and Stacking Fireplace **Wood**

crosswise over the logs and place one or two logs of fair size over all. To start the fire, put paper under the cradle. Fireplace wood should be seasoned at least one year; green wood is hard to ignite and smokes excessively, but a green log may be used as a backlog so that the fire does not burn out too quickly.

SMOOTH SURFACE FIREPLACE

A stone fireplace plastered smooth as shown *(fig. 134)*, and having a wooden mantel, makes a room lined with knotty pine more interesting and cozy. Of course, there should be a beamed ceiling, and sunken hearth for the fire andirons.

The floor is made of flagstones. A rest over the fireplace for display of a favorite firearm increases the rustic effect.

Fig. 134   Smooth Surface Fireplace

Chapter 16

WATER AND SEWERAGE

A water supply that provides a sufficient amount for family use and is still within the scope of the owner's budget is one of the principal problems of the cabin owner.

A sanitary disposal of sewage and other household waste is important, and special precautions will therefore be necessary in making installations to keep the system reasonably free of trouble.

Many states and counties have health departments from which advice and copies of local regulations can be obtained. Study of the problems involved should always precede the spending of money for labor or equipment.

PIONEER WELL

A well made of field stones and cemented together is shown in *fig. 135*, with a watershed over it to prevent rain from entering the well. A windlass is made from a 6-inch round log, to which one end of a rope is fastened, a wooden bucket being fastened on the other end. This type of bucket is made extra heavy and not built like the ordinary wooden pail, otherwise it would have to be replaced too often. The handle of the windlass is made of iron and keyed with a cotter pin on the tang that is inserted into the end of the windlass. A cuff ring is put over each end of the windlass to prevent the ends from cracking, and washers are placed on each side of the post holes. If this well is placed in a sandy region with about 4 feet of the well bottom placed in a dry wall style, the water will seep through and keep the well filled with water. The depth of a well depends on the extent to which you may have to go in order to find water. If entering an old well by ladder or other means, be sure to send down a caged bird or hen first. Gases sometimes form in old wells making them dangerous.

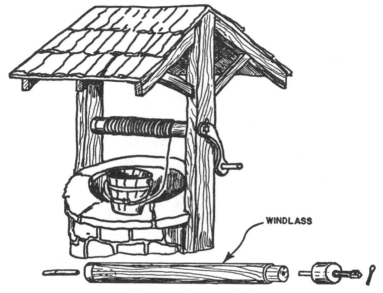

Fig. 135   Pioneer Well

KITCHEN PUMP AND SINK

The old time box sink, enclosed in a framework under which the pots and pans are stored, is still used in many rural farm homes. The sink drainpipe is connected to a cesspool or drainage system whereby the waste water is disposed of. The cover of the sink is a 1¼-inch white pine board with a drainboard on one end and a cut-out for the sink, which fits snugly underneath. Soft glazier's putty is squeezed firmly against it when it is nailed down. The under side of the drainboard and inside of the framework should have three coats of paint to preserve it. The drainboard which has ⅜-inch grooved trenches in it to permit water to drain freely should be covered with three coats of linseed oil and turpentine which is mixed half and half so it will penetrate into the wood. This oiling procedure should be

Fig. 136   Kitchen Pump and Sink

repeated every month until a hard glossy finish is obtained. The pump, which has a pitcher spout, is placed at the right side of the sink, and is bolted down to the top of the sink cover. This type of house pump is usually connected to a cistern or tank and has a suction lift of approximately 25 feet. The diameter of the cylinder is 3 inches and stroke of piston rod is 4 inches. The capacity of a 1¼-inch suction pipe is .12 gallon for each stroke. The cost of this pump is approximately $20 to $25 for an iron cylinder. *(Fig. 136.)*

OUTSIDE FORCE PUMP

These pumps are quite reasonable in price but can be used only for a well which has a depth of 30 feet or less. They are made with a bearer top and air chamber tube and can be operated by hand or windmill. *(Fig. 137.)*

In a pump of this type the top can be revolved to the desired position for the handle and is set with a screw. The top of the rod has a hole in it for the windmill or overhead gasoline engine, so it can be used as a mechanical pump. An outlet is provided back of the spout for a 1¼-inch iron pipe connection to tank or pipe line. A brass gland is used around the pump rod with suitable packing and the handle can be adjusted to strokes of 6, 8, or 9 inches. The cockspout is used for filling a tank or for forcing the water some distance, but should the spout be used for a pail or container the cock is left open. The size of the cylinder is 3 inches by 10 inches, with a 6-inch stroke, and a 1¼-inch

Fig. 137   Force Pump

suction pipe will supply a capacity of .18 gallon per stroke. This type of pump costs approximately $35, installation and freight being extra. If a brass lined cylinder is desired the cost would be approximately $10 additional.

WATER SOURCE

A small creek can be utilized as a source of drinking water if the water is filtered by passing through a bed of clean stone and sand. Sinking of a well by a well driller is usually best, but the well sometimes turns out to be dry. If any type of stream is available, a back-log of water can be made by damming up the stream as shown in *fig. 138*.

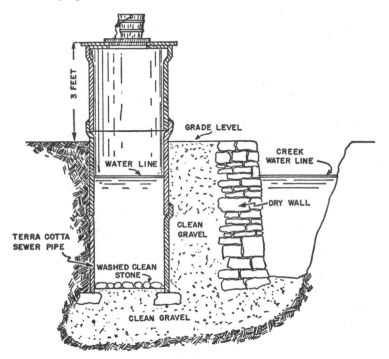

Fig. 138 Filtered Drinking Water

A well made of terra cotta pipe, with a sand and stone bottom and path from the water source should be sufficient for a small family. The piping should be 2 to 3 feet in diameter. Concrete pipe 2 to 3 feet in diameter can be used, but the terra cotta is inclined to be cleaner. The well should be deep enough to hold several weeks' supply of water in case the creek should go dry because of summer heat or lack of rain. A dry wall of stone is set against the creek wall. Very little cement is used for its construction, and clean gravel is placed between the well and the wall. The well should have the tile joints sealed so that no drainage from surface water can seep into the well to pollute it. The well's supply of water should come up through the sand from the bottom to insure

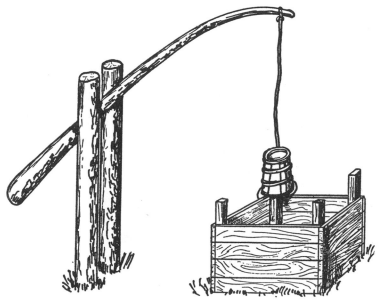

Fig. 139   Dummy Well

proper filtering. The bottom pipe should rest on three large flat stones, and the entire bottom should be lined with clean stones. This will prevent the water from becoming cloudy when the bucket strikes the bottom.

DUMMY WELL

To give a pioneer appearance to the surroundings, a dummy well might be made. The two posts, held together by a long ¾-inch bolt, are set into the ground to hold the hoisting boom. Such a well can be built of any of various types of corners, or stone, or built as shown *(fig. 139)* with slabs nailed to four corner posts. A bucket should be left on the post to make it appear that the well is being used. The lower end of the boom should be heavy enough to keep the rope end of the boom up in the air.

DRIVING THE WELL

After the well has been driven and it is found that enough water can be derived from it to meet every need, the well caisson can be built around it. The pump pipes should be placed to one side of the well so that there will be room to work with a wrench when screwing pipes together. The well

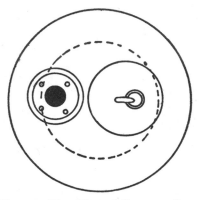

Fig. 140   Top View of Concrete Cover

caisson can be made of field stone, brick, or large vitrified sewer pipes. To cover the well build an 8-inch concrete slab reinforced with ½-inch rods, having brass bolts or thread hooked rods imbedded in the raised section where the pump base is to be placed. A manhole built of concrete or steel should be placed on the top to allow for inspection or repairs that may be needed at any time. A rubber gasket should be placed under the pump base. *(Figs. 140 and 141.)*

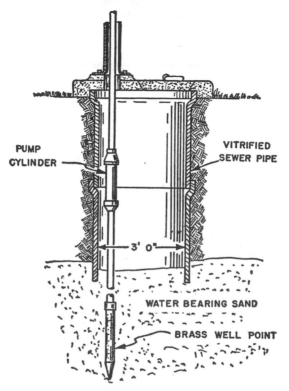

PUMP CYLINDER

VITRIFIED SEWER PIPE

3' 0"

WATER BEARING SAND

BRASS WELL POINT

Fig. 141 Driven Well

No water from pump overflow or surface seepage should be allowed to enter the well at any time. The pump cylinder should be 5 feet below the well surface to prevent freezing during the cold winter period; otherwise a cracked cylinder may be the result. In oiling the well machinery, care should be used so no oil will seep into the well and pollute the water. If a deep cribbed or artesian well for better water is wanted, it is best to hire a professional well-digger. He has the equipment and the experience that goes with it, and can build it at a set price per foot.

WELL POINTS

Well points serve a double purpose; they are drill points for driving the pipe into the earth, and the perforations allow the water to enter, once the water level has been reached.

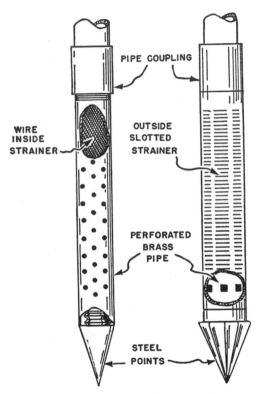

Fig. 142   Points for Driven Well

When well points are driven by a wooden maul into the ground with the hopes of striking a subterranean stream of water or water bearing sand, they should be partly dug first. The points are made of a heavy brass pipe which has holes in it into which the intake of water flows. Over these holes is a brass shield on the outside or the inside of the pipe. These brass shields have a very fine mesh and will not allow large sand particles to enter the pipe through which the water is dispatched to the surface by the action of the pump. The pipe is driven into the ground and if deep enough to allow the pipe to remain partly filled with water at all times, it will help to promote the proper functioning of the pump. Otherwise the pump will need to be primed with water each time it is used.

When starting to drill, attach the point to one end of a 12-foot pipe. A high scaffold should be built to start the drill. On the top end of the pipe a short 18-inch length should be coupled with a cap on it which can be removed. Should the cap or short length split or disfigure when striking, it is a simple matter to replace it. Drive the pipe into the ground until it shows some sign of stopping at a water level. For a test, hook on a small kitchen pump to see if water is obtainable at any level and what amount. Should the project produce a dry well, try to retrieve the point, if not too much trouble, and drill again at another place.

It is good advice not to sink a caisson or crib a well until you have made certain there is water in the well that you have driven. First locate the water and then build the casement. *(Fig. 142.)*

LOG WELL CASING

A log well casing with a water shed to keep out rain, or to give it a pioneer effect, can be built by anyone having a little mechanical ingenuity and ability to use an axe, saw, and hatchet. The logs could be installed over a stone well or used as a dummy for appearance. If the log casing is used over a stone well, the stone well wall must be at least 6 inches above the ground to prevent surface water from seeping into the well. Surface water from rain or other sources may

pollute the drinking water and cause sickness. The shingles
for the roof can be hewn from straight grain timbers about
20 inches long. The shingles can be any width, ⅜ inch to
⅝ inch thick for the bottom, tapering to ⅟₁₆ inch at the
top. *(Fig. 143.)*

Fig. 143   Log Well Casing

CESSPOOL

Figure 144 illustrates a cesspool that is used for disposal
of the home sewage. It can be cleaned whenever necessary,
thus giving the cabin one of the most modern conveniences.
It can be built of concrete, making the walls and floors about

6 inches thick and watertight. The drainage from the roof should not empty into the cesspool as it would fill up with water too quickly. A cesspool should be placed at least 100

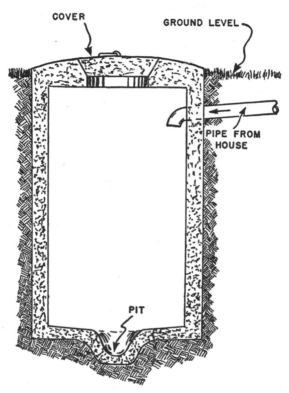

Fig. 144 Concrete Cesspool

feet from a well and below the grade level of the basement floor of the cabin.

If the cabin is in a remote locality the chances are that it will be hard to find anyone to clean out the cesspool. In such a case the use of a septic tank or privy might be the wiser choice.

SEPTIC TANK

This tank can be made of stones plastered on both sides to make it liquid tight, or it can be made of concrete. The sewage is received from the house at one end of the tank and passes into one chamber which is separated from the second chamber by baffle planks with small holes in them. The sewage then passes to the second chamber which also has baffle planks separating it from a third chamber. These first two chambers should have a fairly warm temperature to hasten the bacterial action which is necessary to dispose of some of the solids. The third chamber receives more or less clear fluid which should be drained off in porous concrete pipes that are placed in sand or gravel beds. The clearer liquid can then percolate into the ground. The more piping in the ground, the more liquid the septic tank can dispose of. The solids that are not dispensed with must be cleaned out occasionally. Rain water from roof drains should not empty into a septic tank as the tank will be filled to its capacity after every rainstorm. *(Fig. 145.)*

DISTRIBUTION FIELD

Hard glazed sewer tile should be used to carry the sewage one hundred feet from the house before it has an open joint. The sewage tile used in the distribution field can be ordinary drainage tile left with an open joint. At the joints a piece of heavy roofing paper is placed on top, covering it only on the upper half. This will allow any liquid to drain between each section of tile. When a number of trenches are dug for the distribution field they should be placed in a sandy soil area with the trenches not less than 8 feet apart.

When placing the drain tile in position use screened pebbles ranging from ¾ inch to 3 inches in diameter in the bottom. Then lay the drain tile on top, sloping it at not less than ¼

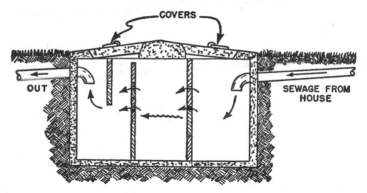

Fig. 145   Septic Tank

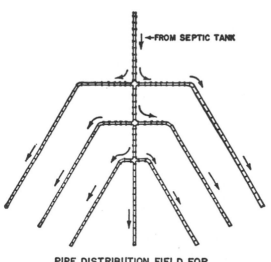

PIPE DISTRIBUTION FIELD FOR
LIQUID DRAINAGE

Fig. 146   *Left,* Drainage Tile; *right,* Concrete Porous Drainage Tile

inch per foot. The greater the length of piping, the greater amount of sewage that can be disposed of. Place the distribution field so its outlet, if any, will not seep to the surface and contaminate drinking water. A concrete porous tile can be made by half "U" sections, one on top and one on the bottom. The material is ¼-inch pebbles only, and screening of fine sand equivalent to house screen mesh. A mixture of one part cement, one of sand, and five of ¼-inch pebbles, just wet enough so the pebbles are merely coated, will make a porous pipe. There are porous concrete drainage tile on the market as shown in the illustration. *(Fig. 146.)*

PIPE TRENCH

This illustration *(fig. 147)* shows an end view of the distribution pipe trench. It must be dug deeper in a cold cli-

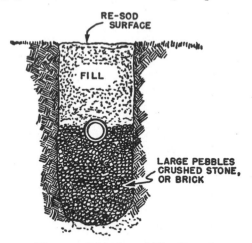

Fig. 147   End View of Pipe Trench

mate than in a mild climate to prevent freezing. A depth of 18 inches is sufficient in mild climates whereas in climates where the frost line will extend to a depth of 3 feet the trench should be of the same depth. The deeper the stone filter cushion the greater its capacity to absorb liquid. Large pebbles, crushed stone, or brick can be used. Top soil should be saved to recover; also the surface sod can be relaid. The width of the trench depends on whether it is clay or sandy soil. If in sandy soil, the trench need not be any wider than you can walk in, but in a clay soil the trench percolating surface may depend entirely on the gravel or cushion material for its functioning purpose. A width of from 18 inches to 2 feet may be desired.

OUTDOOR PRIVY

The building of an outdoor privy is important if no other sanitary means is provided. It is best to keep the privy away from stream or lake so that it will not pollute the water in which there may be swimming or boating. The trench should first be dug about 5 feet deep and then cribbed up with 1-inch by 8-inch boards to the grade level. The next step is to place two logs about 8 inches in diameter along the trench upon which the floor is built. The frame for the sides and roof is next built up of 2-inch by 4-inch logs, and the roof is covered with shiplap or 5-plyboard. The door is also made of the same material. A roofing paper is placed on the roof. The four sides are covered with 2-inch and 3-inch saplings which fit tightly together. There are two toilet seats with covers over each. Screens should be placed over the window openings in the sides and door.

The U.S. Department of Agriculture has a booklet which it sells at small cost dealing with disposal of farm sewage. The problems of disposal for a camp are much like those of the farm so this book can be recommended.

A camouflage of lilac bushes or small trees will help dress

up the surroundings, as well as hide the privy. Installations should be made away from and below level of drinking water supply. *(Fig. 148.)*

Fig. 148   Privy Made of 2″ and 3″ Saplings on 2″ x 4″ Frame

Chapter 17

FURNITURE

Much of the enjoyment and beauty of a cabin lies in the interior plus the furniture. A good bed and mattress will give you the proper rest. Furniture, either purchased or home-made, may be neatly set around the fireplace, and one who lives in the city will find it really enchanting to relax there after a hike or work around the cabin. A tinker-kit cabinet-maker may devise any number of new ideas in furniture, or build pieces following magazine pictures and plans to suit his needs. Oddly-made furniture has a value that money cannot always purchase. Try to be original in making some odd piece of furniture (even if others scoff at your ideas) so long as it is something useful.

USING FOX WEDGE

A fox wedge is placed inside the tenon before placing it in the hole and forcing the joint hard up. The glue (casein if it can be had) will cause it to tighten in the hole and keep the wedge from becoming loose. *(Fig. 149.)*

When making furniture or other items of wood, it is very important that the holes for nails and screws be first drilled so that the wood does not split. The top of the hole should be countersunk as this will prevent the wood from splitting, and will keep the head of the nail or screw from catching in one's clothes, or from causing any damage to a person's hand when cleaning.

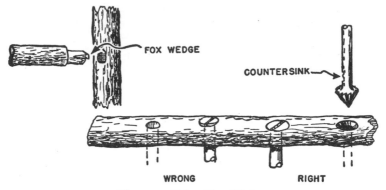

Fig. 149   Using Fox Wedges

GUN HOLDER

A display of guns is the pride of all campers and outdoor people. How to make a simple rack without great expense, is shown here. *(Fig. 150.)* The main sections can be cut in half, with a branch on the bottom for a hook. If a hook for the two bottoms cannot be had in one piece of log, two can

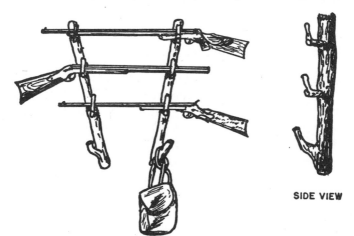

Fig. 150   Wall Gun Rack

be used. The hooks for the gun rests are merely ⅝-inch right angle twigs cut off and forced into holes drilled into the upright piece. A nail is then driven into the upright piece to prevent the twig from coming out or turning around. The rack is nailed or screwed to the side wall.

WASH STAND OR SEAT

A half log dressed by an axe or plane to have a fairly smooth surface can be made into a wash stand or seat. The ground on which the legs rest must be fairly hard, otherwise the legs must be placed on flat stones which serve as a footing. The

Fig. 151   Wash Stand

logs should be sufficiently large to carry the half log and the weight that is expected to be placed upon it. The leg hole should be 2 to 3 inches in diameter and at least 3 inches deep. The leg itself should have a shoulder to prevent the leg from moving deeper into the hole after once set, with a nail driven into the leg by way of the half log, to prevent the leg from becoming loose. *(Fig. 151.)*

BACKWOODS SETTEE

To make a settee of this type, a slab log is required with at least 4 inches at its thickest point. The legs and arms are bored into this slab at various angles and fox wedged or glued together. To be certain that the doweled ends hold, drive a nail near the hole, penetrating into the tenon so the seat legs or back do not become loose. Bore holes for removable handles and insert them on each end when moving the settee. This is much better than moving by lifting with the settee arm which is not usually strong enough for such treatment. *(Fig. 152.)*

WOOD BOX

A wood box 1 foot 4 inches wide and 1 foot 6 inches high (inside measurements) and 2 feet long made from 4-inch slabs of logs can be attractive yet inexpensive. A ⅛-inch by 2-inch iron or brass strap can be fastened around the sides and bottom and joined at the top with a handle which is made from a pipe and bolt. The slab pieces are all doweled together and the bark is removed from all surfaces. The legs are either round or square with dowels fastening them to the bottom. The metal can be painted black and the rest of the wood surface covered with three coats of varnish. *(Fig. 153.)*

OLD DUTCH SETTEE

This shows a table that can be used as a bench and seat. *(Fig. 154.)* The limbs are first peeled and then varnished. This type of table seat was used in early American days and can be converted into a handy piece of furniture as the occasion arises. The bottom is used as a storage bin for shoes, etc. When in use as a seat, it might be placed near a wall.

DOOR KNOCKERS

A door knocker can easily be made by cutting an 8-inch log on the diagonal, leaving a support for the movable knocker. The knocker is made of a twig having a hole drilled into the upper end to receive the cross pin. The appropriate sign is painted on the face after it has been given a coat of varnish.

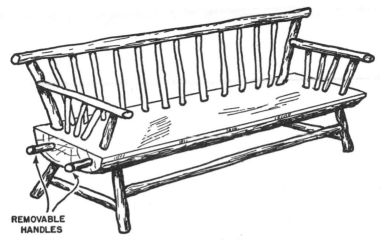

REMOVABLE
HANDLES

Fig. 152 Backwoods Settee

½" BOLT   PIPE HANDLE

Fig. 153 Wood Box

1' 6"

⅛" X 2" STRAP
IRON

1' 4"

CLOSED AND USED
AS A TABLE

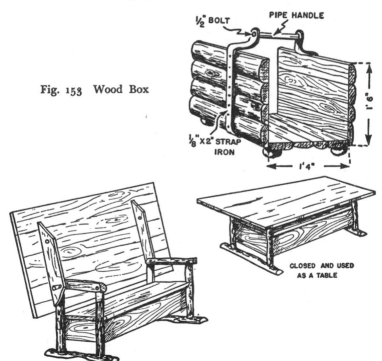

Fig. 154 Old Dutch Settee

Fig. 155   Door Knocker

Three coats of good spar varnish are necessary to make the surface and bark waterproof. Two holes are drilled for oval-headed screws, which hold the knocker to the door. *(Fig. 155.)*

MOVABLE CAMP BED

This type of camp bed can be moved on the ground, to tents or outdoors. It will keep the sleeper off the ground and is fairly comfortable. It is made entirely of two 8-inch runners and saplings stripped of their bark. The advantage of making it in this fashion is that it prevents the woodsman from having to split logs or saplings which require sawing or splitting of the material. The correct size ties can be cut and nailed together with no other tools than a hammer, an axe and a saw. A mattress made from burlap bags or canvas ducking filled with dry leaves or grass can be put on top. *(Fig. 156.)*

CAMP BED

This camp bed is inexpensive and comfortable. *(Fig. 157.)* The framework is made of cleaned 2½-inch trees, braced as shown, and held together with carriage bolts tightly fastened to their proper station. The spring is made of clothesline cord woven to make a mesh approximately 3 inches square. The bed tick can be filled with dried straw or leaves and kept filled so that the cord spring will not be felt. It is important that the

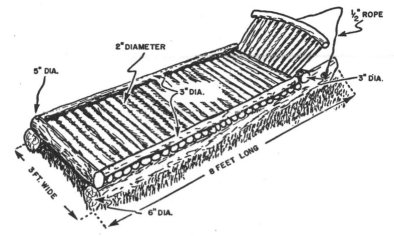

Fig. 156 Movable Camp Bed

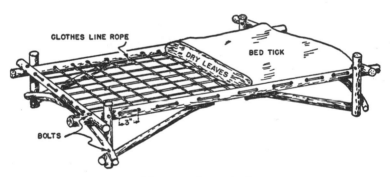

Fig. 157 Camp Bed

leaves be thoroughly dry so they will not turn moldy. A spring of this nature must be properly stretched or one cord will be felt more than the others; this will mean improper rest. A sheet of canvas ducking placed over the cords will make the bunk more satisfactory.

FOLDING CHAIR

A folding chair made from 2½-inch diameter tree limbs is not only comfortable but practical. The frame should be

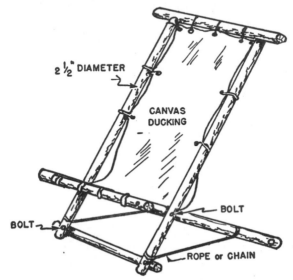

2 ½" DIAMETER

CANVAS
DUCKING

BOLT

BOLT

ROPE or CHAIN

Fig. 158   Folding Chair

cleaned of all bark and stained or varnished. Eyelets around the edges of the canvas are used to strap it to the frame. A chain or rope holds the inclining back at a suitable angle. This chair can be folded up to occupy a small space in a storage room. *(Fig. 158.)*

LIGHTING FIXTURES

Fig. 159. "A" shows how an old wagon wheel can be utilized as a fixture with a candle set in a steel or brass socket which holds a glass lamp chimney.

"B" shows an electrical fixture which is also made with the wagon wheel, and with the shade hanging from the lower side

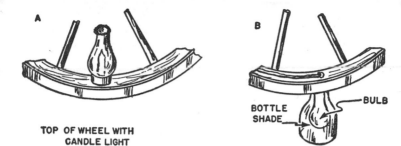

A

TOP OF WHEEL WITH
CANDLE LIGHT

B

BOTTLE SHADE

BULB

Fig. 159   Electric Fixture

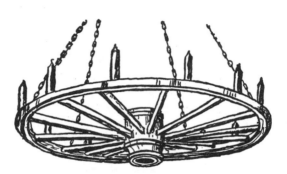

Fig. 160   Light Fixture

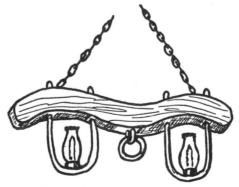

Fig. 161   Yoke Light Fixture

of the wheel. An old large-necked bottle which has the bottom cut out can be used. Many varieties of old-time green, brown or blue bottles make excellent fixtures and are also cheap.

In *fig. 160* candles fastened into holes in the wheel just for appearance make an interesting fixture.

Fig. 161 shows how two old kitchen chair backs can be utilized as an antique fixture resembling an ox yoke, with sockets that hold both the candles and glass lamp chimneys.

DE LUXE CHAISE

A comfortable rest can be made from two wheels, 1½-inch lumber for the frame, a hank or so of clothesline cord, a cross rod for the wheel and two strap hinges. The cushion can be

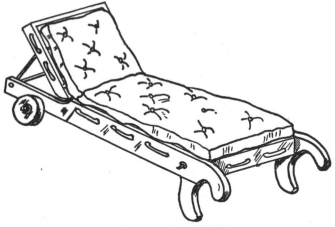

Fig. 162   De Luxe Chaise

made of canvas ducking filled with straw, or some better filler if desired. It should be fairly well filled so the cords will not be felt when lying down on the cushion. It is better to make the cushion in two sections, one for the head and one for the flat. *(Fig. 162.)*

CLUB CHAIR AND LOVE SEAT

These are made of the same kind of material and in the same way as the chaise lounge, but the arm rests can be made of 1-inch lumber. A cross rod for the legs can be made of ½-inch iron, and the cushion should be made in two sections. The cushions can be painted or coated with an oil that will dry, or made of waterproof canvas to protect them from possible rain damage. A custom-made covering that will stand up in all weather conditions can be bought from seat upholstery establishments for a nominal cost. *(Figs. 163 and 164.)*

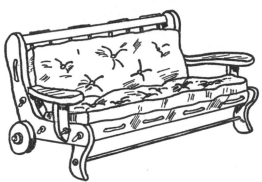

Fig. 163   Love Seat

Fig. 164   Club Chair

Chapter 18

CARE OF CABIN AND GROUNDS

CARE WILL EXTEND THE LIFE OF YOUR CABIN

One who owns a log cabin which has the bark left on the logs is apt to discover that in a short time the cabin's beauty has begun to fade because of the bark falling off. When he starts to peel all the bark off he may discover that during the time since the building of the cabin he has harbored millions of unwanted insects (tree borers), and that they have marred the surface of the log next to the bark. A warning to peel and creosote the logs before building is advice well worth heeding. Insects cause considerable damage to unpeeled logs of the principal woods used in construction of log cabins. This damage, which varies from the numerous small holes in the bark to the complete destruction of the heartwood, causes annoyance and unsightly condition of material.

When logs show holes with a loose wood powder in or around them, there is no doubt a tree borer or beetle at work. D.D.T. insecticide can be used in a small-mouthed spray to exterminate this pest, and a careful vigilance on all wood-destroying insects should be kept at all times to preserve the life of the cabin. Logs that lie on the ground or are closest to it are especially subject to decay or infection by wood-destroying insects.

As the timbers dry out there is a shrinkage due to cracks developing as they get older. These cracks should be well saturated with creosote and filled with a calking compound as soon as possible to prolong the life of the timber. Leakage of the roof, or other damages which cause dampness in the cabin, should not be neglected as dry timbers outlast all others. Log cabins have stood for sixty years, but the life of a cabin depends on the care it receives.

TIN TREE SHIELD

A tin shield placed around a tree will prevent squirrels from stealing food from a bird shelter, and also prevent bobcats from sucking eggs and killing all types of birds. Squirrels have been known to jump 8 feet from limb to limb, so a tree with a bird nest, bird house, or shelter, must have its limbs cut so it will at no time be near other trees, or else shields must be placed around the trunks of all trees in a group. Large tin cans with the top and bottom removed can have seams trimmed and be beaten to curve around a tree, painting them when they get rusty, lapping the joints, and nailing them together with galvanized roofing nails. (*Fig. 165.*)

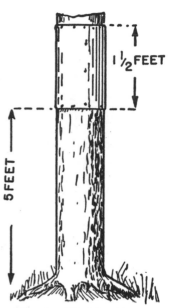

Fig. 165   Tin Tree Shield

GIRDLING A TREE

A quick method of planting corn or vegetables in the forest without cutting down the trees was taught the pioneers by the Indians. Plant your seeds among the trees in the regular manner. Use a hand axe to cut the bark off the trees about 18 inches wide all around, making certain that you cut into the tree beneath the bark. By this method, called "girdling," the tree will lose all its leaves and die, with merely the limbs standing. This will allow the sun to penetrate to the planted vegetables and will enable one to raise a crop which may be needed while the cabin is being built, without

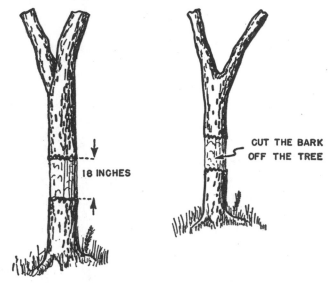

Fig. 166   Girdling a Tree to Kill It

having to stop to clear the land for a much needed crop. The trees can be cut down during the winter or at a time when one has a few days to accomplish the tree felling. *(Fig. 166.)*

TRIMMING TREE FOR BEAUTY

When stubs are left on a tree a few suckers may sprout at its base, which grow faster than any other part of the tree. Stubs usually die back to the succeeding branches, thus causing rot to develop, which moves downward through the limb to the trunk, sometimes killing the tree. Cuts should be covered with tree paint or a heavy paint mixed with linseed oil. *(Fig. 167.)*

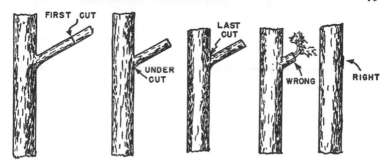

Fig. 167   Trimming Tree for Beauty

REMOVABLE FENCE

A panel fence that can be stored away in the winter is pictured here. *(Fig. 168.)* The posts, which are creosoted, are left in the ground. They should be painted in the fall and again in the spring when the fence panels are painted. The holes in the fence should be 1¼ inches in diameter and the dowel pins, which are made of wood, should be 1 inch in diameter. The length of the dowel pin depends upon the size of the posts and the panel fence side style posts. The dowel pins should extend 3 inches inside the panel post; this provides the novelty effect. The bottom rail should be 1 foot from the ground to allow cutting of the grass with a lawn mower. The permanent fence posts should stand 4 feet above the ground and be set 2 feet into the ground. If a smaller fence is desired, perhaps as a lawn novelty fence, it must be remembered that the measurements should be in correct proportion.

RAIL FENCE

A fence of cut timber merely crossed at the ends, as shown *(fig. 169)*, makes a simple fence that will keep out livestock. It lends a pioneer appearance to cabin surroundings. The timber should be wedged split rails, piled criss-cross about

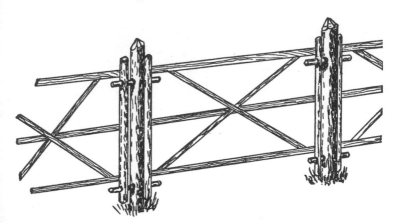

Fig. 168   Removable Fence Panels

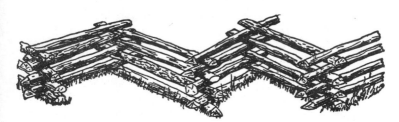

Fig. 169   Rail Fence

Fig. 170   Snake Fence

6 inches to 10 inches from the ends. The fence can be built up to a height of 5 feet for use as a windbreak in the winter, and can be used for firewood by taking off timber from the top. The rails should be about 10 to 12 feet long.

SNAKE FENCE

A snake fence can be built of small tree limbs about 3 to 6 inches in diameter, or of split rails. This type of fence was used in early pioneer days and gives the surroundings a regular Yankee appearance. Each forked section is approximately 10 feet apart, and bolted or nailed together. The bark should be removed from the limbs which should be soaked in creosote to preserve them. Care should be taken to prevent grass fires, which may mean the end of the fence. *(Fig. 170.)*

DECORATIVE FENCE

This type of fence can be built by anyone having a little knowledge of mechanics. The holes in the posts can be cut out with a 1-inch wood drill; three holes are drilled side by side and the material between them cut out with a wood chisel. The distance between the holes, center to center, should be approximately 10 inches. The first hole should be about 8 inches from the ground. After all the horizontal bars have been set in place the center upright and diagonal strips should be secured by drilling with a gimlet drill and fastening with brass stove bolts. The bark should be stripped from the saplings and the posts hewn out to give a more realistic effect. Elmwood is not satisfactory for this work as it is not only hard to work with, but its wavy grain makes it difficult to use. The posts can be placed into the ground any distance desired as this fence is used for decorative purposes only. *(Fig. 171.)*

Fig. 171   Decorative Fence

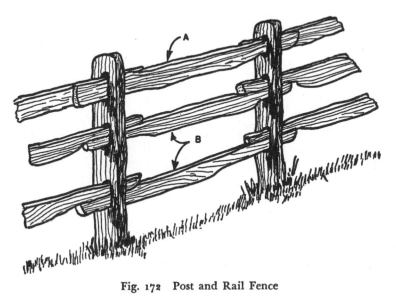

Fig. 172   Post and Rail Fence

POST AND RAIL FENCE

A fence of this type is made from split rails and requires a great deal of splitting and drilling of holes. If only a short stretch is wanted for decorative purposes, this project can be done in a cellar and installed on the grounds.

(Fig. 172.) "A" shows an example of a side-by-side method of splicing. "B" illustrates, on the center and bottom rails, a type of top and bottom splicing. Either method gives a neat appearance, but the author believes the "A" method to be the stronger of the two.

GATE ENTRANCE

This gate with its overhead rustic canopy supplies a very realistic pioneer appearance. *(Fig. 173.)* All the saplings and posts should be peeled and soaked with creosote and kerosene to give them a long life. Two posts are set up 8 feet apart and stand about 8 feet above the ground, with at least 3 feet in the ground. A 4-foot cross member on each post is braced on each side. Two rafters on each side are fitted and placed together with a tie brace on each span. Two-inch saplings are then nailed on top. These are not meant to be waterproof, but simply to improve the appearance. The gate is made 3 feet wide, hinged between with two posts. A rustic sapling fence is then placed between the gate posts and larger posts on each side, the tops tapering up to the regular height of the rustic sapling fence.

SAPLING FENCE

This drawing shows a fence made from saplings to any height desired. *(Fig. 174.)* A post can be placed every 8 feet to support the fence. The saplings are peeled of their bark, soaked over night in creosote diluted with kerosene and woven the same as ordinary cloth is woven with a double

Fig. 173   Gate Entrance

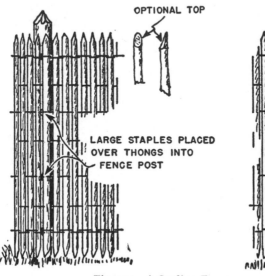

OPTIONAL TOP

LARGE STAPLES PLACED
OVER THONGS INTO
FENCE POST

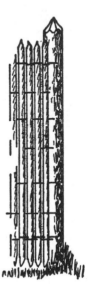

Fig. 174   A Sapling Fence

string of thongs on the top and bottom. The sapling in a fence should not be over 1½ inches in diameter after being peeled. If there is no one to take care of the property during the winter months this type of fence should be taken down every fall as a precaution against damage by grass fires and heavy snows. This fence is more decorative than practical for a long durable life and needs plenty of care.

WEAVING LOOM RACK

A rack for weaving a sapling fence or for making a curtain from wands is shown here. *(Fig. 175.)* Two rows of stakes are driven into the ground and the thongs tied to them about 18 inches from the ground. The weaving thongs are also tied

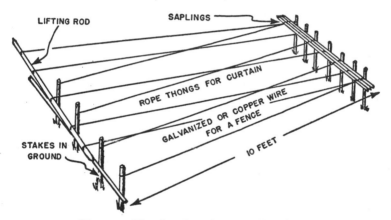

Fig. 175   Weaving Curtain or Sapling Fence

to one row of stakes and the opposite end tied to a lifting rod 1½ feet beyond the end stakes. As the saplings or wands are woven into the object, the thongs on the lifting cross bar are raised or lowered between the stake-tied thongs. The saplings or wands must be kept close to each other for a tight fence or screen. Light cotton or hemp rope should be used for wands on a screen as this is more suitable for folding up

Willow

Fir

Pin Oak

Silver Maple

Birch

Red Maple

Redwood

Hickory

Fig. 176

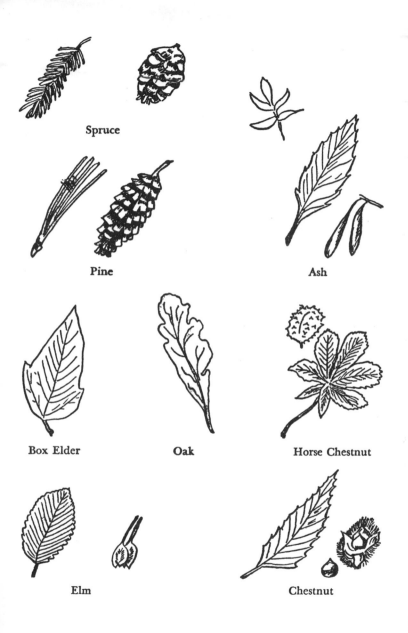

Spruce

Pine

Ash

Box Elder

Oak

Horse Chestnut

Elm

Chestnut

or storage in a small space. Galvanized or copper bale wire is suitable for a fence, but galvanized wire will outlast the fence. If the weight of the object makes the thongs sag, a support can be placed underneath during the process of making. A fence of this type can be rolled up and stored away in sections.

IDENTIFICATION OF TREE LEAVES

When the knowledge of trees is limited any individual who is not a woodsman can learn to tell a tree by its fallen leaves or its bark. The following illustrations of leaves *(fig. 176)* will help to identify a tree, as the leaves do not fall far away. If there is snow on the ground remove the snow and scrape the ground until a leaf can be found. Only a skilled woodsman can identify a tree by its bark.

Chapter 19

MISCELLANEOUS

LOW CULVERTS

When a roadway must be built over a small stream a low culvert made from heavy timbers, as shown *(fig. 177)*, serves the purpose very well. Stone must be laid for the bed, or water will undermine the bottom. The culvert is made approximately 3 feet wide and 2 feet high inside. The cross timbers should be made of 6-inch diameter timber or logs. The side timbers can be butt joints, but should be fairly tight.

CORDUROY ROAD

Where a road runs over a swampy section or low ground that has no drainage, the road tends to soften. The simplest and cheapest method of building and keeping the road usable is known as corduroying the road. Limbs about 2 to 4 inches in diameter are suitable for the bottom layer. Of course, larger diameter limbs could be used, but the larger timber can be used to better advantage in the building of the cabin. Limbs trimmed off the cabin logs can also be used under the bottom timbers. The larger saplings help hold the dirt and gravel fill in place. Road curb timbers are placed on the sides of the road and held in place by 3-inch stakes driven into the marshy ground to a depth of about 2 feet. The fill is made up of large stones approximately 2 inches in diameter, coarse gravel, and then the road fill which may be either dirt or sand. The thickness of the fill depends largely on what is

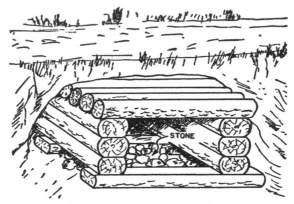

Fig. 177   Low Strong Culvert

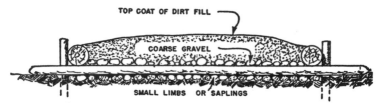

TOP COAT OF DIRT FILL

COARSE GRAVEL

SMALL LIMBS   OR   SAPLINGS

Fig. 178   Cross Section of Corduroy Road

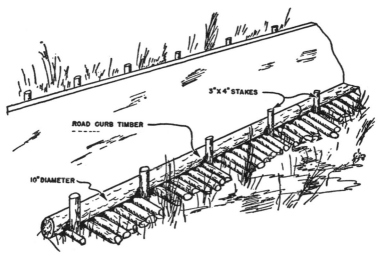

3"X 4" STAKES

ROAD CURB TIMBER

10" DIAMETER

Fig. 179   Corduroy Road

available in the vicinity. When complete, the fill should weigh the twigs down to an even roadbed as illustrated here. *(Figs. 178 and 179.)*

BELL POST

A post with a fair sized bell placed under a small protective roof, with a rope bell pull which is approximately 5 feet off the ground, is a novelty and yet could be used for assembly or dinner call in camp, as well as in case of fire. This type can be built on a single post mortised and tenoned to cross pieces and supports as shown *(fig. 180)*, making it strong as well as unique in design. The first rung is placed 5 feet off the ground to prevent small children from climbing on it. The bell should be a ship's bell about 10 inches in diameter.

SIGN POST

A sign post for a camp or home in the woods adds a little dignity to the place. The upright post is 8 inches in diameter at the bottom, about 13 feet long, and placed in the ground to a depth of 3 feet, after being creosoted. The cross member and back brace are about 6 inches in diameter. The cross member is cut half way into the post and bolted. The brace is mortised and tenoned into the post and cross brace and doweled with two $\frac{3}{8}$-inch dowels in each end. The sign which is held by $\frac{1}{4}$-inch screw eyes, should not hang lower than $6\frac{1}{2}$ feet above the ground. The ends of the sign should be rough cut and the surface given five coats of varnish, two coats before the sign is painted and three afterwards. If the sign is to be made in pieces, they should be doweled together. *(Fig. 181.)*

REMOVABLE SIGN

A signboard, as shown *(fig. 182)*, is placed between two permanent posts set in the ground and removed by unscrew-

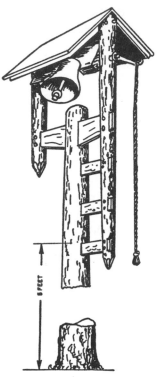

Fig. 181   Sign Post

Fig. 182   Removable Sign

Fig. 180   Bell Post

ing from the horizontal bars. The posts should be 8 inches in diameter and 9 feet long, and stripped of the bark. The horizontal bars and sign are stored and repainted each season to keep them looking neat and to preserve them for a long time. The permanent posts should be saturated in creosote after they have been thoroughly dried and seasoned. After they have been holed they can be placed at least 4 feet into the ground. They are preserved by applying a heavy coat of creosote in the spring and fall. If used in the Pacific coast area the posts should be coated in the fall, again before the rainy season starts in January, and again in April.

RUSTIC BRIDGE

A rustic bridge of pleasing appearance, yet durable and strong is illustrated here. *(Fig. 183.)* The side retaining walls

Fig. 183   Log Bridge

are made of logs or stone, bolted or strongly anchored into the side banks. The cross beams are made of 10-inch diameter logs placed close together the entire length of the bridge plus 3 feet on each end. A 3-inch planking is placed on the timbers over the beams lain crosswise. Rails are placed on uprights, as shown, with diagonal bracing to stiffen them against outward motion. The horizontal supports for the diagonal braces extend the entire width of the bridge and are cut half way through to act as a plank at this point. The log should be peeled and saturated thoroughly with creosote. The planks and timbers of the roadway should be soaked in a solution of creosote and tar to prevent insects from destroying them.

LARGE CULVERT IN GULLEY

This type of culvert is a makeshift affair and can be used temporarily until a more permanent type can be built. A long timber rests on forked timbers as shown, using as many

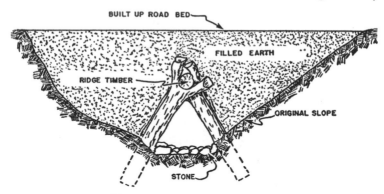

Fig. 184   Large Lean-to Culvert

as can possibly be found with a crotch. The crotch timbers are set into the ground about 2 feet deep. The remainder of the slant wall is made with lean-to timbers and twigs set so close together that no earth fill will be washed through by water that might seep through. The top fill is made of dirt and the bottom between the logs is filled with stone to keep the bottom from closing up or from washing out. *(Fig. 184.)*

TIMBER BRIDGE

A strong bridge for heavy loads can be built by imbedding logs into both banks and filling in the cribbing with logs at 4-foot intervals, then spiking or trunneling them together with wooden pegs. The road level should have the bed logs close enough together to hold the stone and earth fill, and a skirt timber 16 inches in diameter on each side of the road-way to hold the road fill in place. The stones should be no larger than 1½ inches, screened and packed neatly, with asphaltic spray if it can be had in the locality. Asphaltic spray is emulsified asphalt diluted in water and sprayed from a common garden sprinkler. The holes in the sprinkler should be opened to the size of an 8-penny nail as they gradually close by coagulation. Kerosene should be used to clean the sprinkler, and it can then be washed. *(Fig. 185.)*

RUSTIC GARDEN BRIDGE

A decorative bridge crossing a small creek or pool can be easily built of curved trees. Three or four curved timbers of about the same length are held together by cross planking, or by 4-foot limbs that are 3 to 4 inches wide. Holes for all spikes should be drilled and 40- or 60-penny nails used to obtain a good solid fastening. The planking should be peeled of bark and heavily creosoted to make it last longer. The ends of the bridge should be imbedded in the shore line to a depth of at least 1 foot and braced against stone. The hand rail should be fastened to the bridge stringer and rail post with 6-inch by ⅜-inch lag screws. Lilies and cattails can be planted in the pool. *(Fig. 186.)*

Fig. 185 Timber Bridge Over a Small Creek

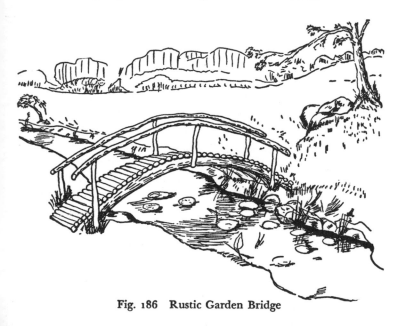

Fig. 186 Rustic Garden Bridge

MAIL BOX HOLDER

A log 8 inches thick, with a Y-shaped fork at one end can be made into an ideal mail box holder. The bark should be peeled off, the log soaked in a barrel of creosote for a week to saturate thoroughly, and then imbedded 3 feet in the ground. Creosoting will give it a longer life. The top should

Fig. 187　Mail Box Holder

be cut level and a 1-inch board should be laid on top and nailed securely to the log. The mail box is then screwed to the board. Place the log slanting toward the road in order that the mailman may place the mail in the box while still sitting in his auto or buggy. The post may be set 6 feet back from the road line, but this is not so convenient for the mailman. Place stones around the bottom of the post in such a way that road traffic will not travel too close to the post. *(Fig. 187.)*

BUCKING BARREL OR LOG

This is a 7-foot log or a common barrel about 18 inches in diameter and suspended 40 inches off the ground to its top. The bucking log is held by four ⅝-inch hemp ropes held in

Fig. 188   Bucking Log

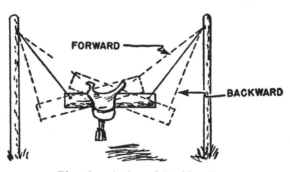

Fig. 189   Action of Bucking Log

a diagonal position. These ropes are fastened to four posts which are imbedded in the ground about 5 feet. A saddle is held fast on the middle of the log. By moving the log forward and backward, a movement similar to that of a trotting or bucking horse is obtained. When the ropes are pulled forward, the log end goes forward and down and the after end rises. When the movement goes backward, the after end goes down and the forward end goes up. This action is more like the real action of horseback riding than anything yet devised, as shown in the illustration of the action of the bucking log. *(Figs. 188 and 189.)*

DUG-OUT CANOE

To make a dug-out a large timber with clear wood and no decayed heart growth must be found. A timber about 16 feet long and 36 inches in diameter is about right, and it should be of white oak, cedar, white pine, spruce, or cypress.

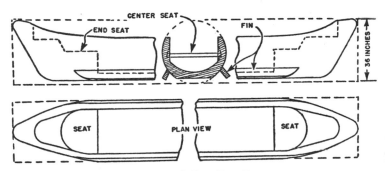

Fig. 190   A Log Dug-Out

To dig out the inside of a canoe the craftsman should use a large wooden drill to simplify the work and keep all the tools sharp. A wooden mallet, broad chisel, inside- and outside-beveled gouge chisel, and a 1-inch flat chisel are needed. Do not force the inside outward when at either end of the dug-out, otherwise there is danger of splitting the end sides, thus causing the dug-out to leak. Leave plenty of tumble-home on the side to steady the rolling action, and nail two fin keels on the bottom for protection. Spruce, white

pine, and cypress are lighter and easier to dig out than white
oak. If the dug-out has a tendency to capsize, place a steel
bar on it as a keel. This will give the dug-out more stability.
(Fig. 190.)

DAMS

What is a camp without its swimming hole? By this I mean
to say you do not get the complete satisfaction of a camping
vacation unless you have one. *Figs. 191–196* show various

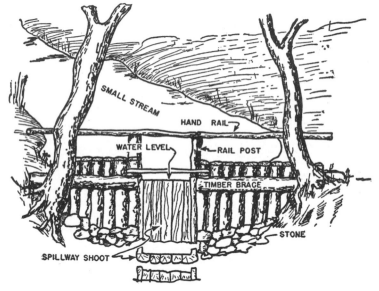

Fig. 191

dams that can be built in woodland streams or along stony
creeks to raise the water enough for swimming, or even
small-time boating. Small creeks not any larger than a mere
trickle can be built up to make a sizable little pond if a
proper selection of place and workmanship is possible. A
creek, regardless of how small, may be turned into a stream

during a rainstorm, and if held in check by a dam and puri-fied during every rainstorm, can bring quite a lot of enjoy-ment to young and old alike. This can best be done in a

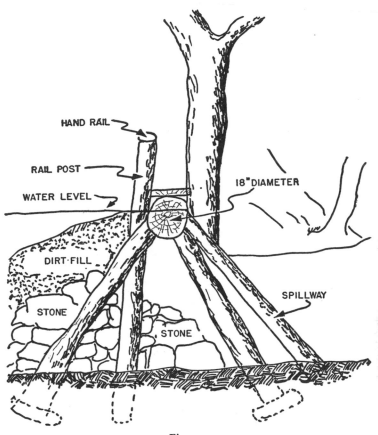

Fig. 192

ravine where the backing up of water may not have any damaging effect on the surrounding countryside.

Timber must be plentiful if the dam is to be made of wood. If not, loose stones can be used, the overflow height being made the depth of the water wanted. The space where the pond is desired should be cleaned before filling as it would be much harder to clean when full of water. All stumps, sharp and jagged stones, and any obstacles that may cut or injure a person's feet must be removed. Loose leaves should be raked out and rotten timbers removed, and, if a sandy bottom can be made, it should be done then and not after the pond is filled, unless the pond can be drained at will. Do not burn the leaves and let the ashes lie in the pond bottom. The leaves, grass, etc. can be utilized by sprinkling sparingly in the loose dirt fill which is necessary to keep it from being washed away by a heavy downpour.

Fig. 191 shows how a swimming hole can be built in a ravine, the main support of timbers resting against an 18-inch large timber which has been lodged against two trees, one on each side. This gives a good backstop and one that will not be washed away very easily. The other upright timbers are dug into the dirt bed about 3 feet below the bottom so the water at no time will undermine the dam.

Fig. 192 shows the side view of a cut section and the method of bracing the spillway and the upper side. A small hand rail is set on top to allow crossing by foot on the cross timber.

Fig. 193. This type of dam is built of two rows of upright timbers set deep in the ground, about 5 feet apart. A dirt fill is required between the rows of timbers so it takes a little more work and skill than the other dams. The timbers must be set together tightly and calked with old unraveled rope strands. The top cross timbers are lodged against a large boulder or post dug deep into the ground.

Fig. 194 shows the cut view and the spillway for the overflow, which should be of stones laid in concrete. Cementing the stones will prevent relaying of them after every downpour. The two rows of timbers should be held together by ⅝-inch galvanized tie rods placed every 4 feet along the large

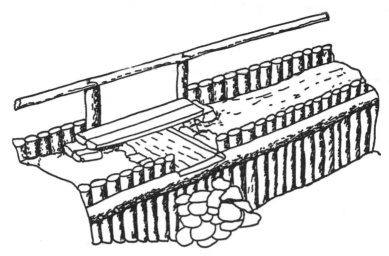

Fig. 193

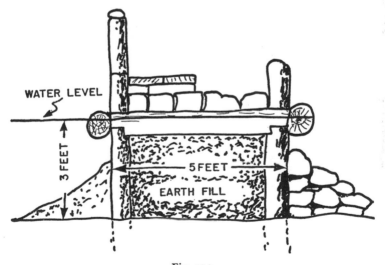

WATER LEVEL

3 FEET

5 FEET

EARTH FILL

Fig. 194

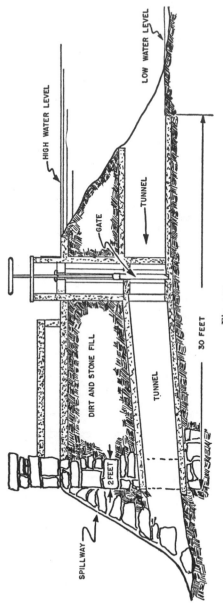

HIGH WATER LEVEL

LOW WATER LEVEL

TUNNEL

GATE

TUNNEL

30 FEET

DIRT AND STONE FILL

SPILLWAY

2 FEET

Fig. 195

cross timbers. A hand rail is placed on the upper side and a two-plank walk over the spillway. This is not meant for a big stream or a deep one, merely as a small duck or wading pool not over 5 feet deep.

Fig. 195 shows a large dam with a stone reclining wall. This can be utilized for water power to a small extent and represents the best dam shown. A 2-foot thick stone wall which is made heavier at the bottom is placed in the after side. A valve gate or a sluice gate can be used to stop the water from passing through the tunnel at any time. The dirt fill is then launched against the upward side of the dam to a top width of 15 feet. A 10-foot wide spillway and overflow is recessed in the top to a depth of 2 feet. The spillway is made of concrete, as is the tunnel. This dam is approximately 15 feet high.

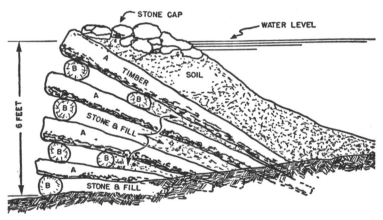

Fig. 196

Fig. 196. A timber and stone dam may be made of stone, beams, straw and timber placed as shown, and imbedded deep enough into the stream bed so it will not be washed away. The timbers should be fastened together with ⅝-inch iron rods by drilling a hole into both members the same size as the rod to tie the unit together. Large square galvanized spikes can be used though they are expensive. A certain amount of water will seep through this dam but it will answer the purpose until a better one can be built. The stones on top at the lowest point will act as a spillway surface and prevent too much earth from washing away.

If you are the dark-skinned type you will tan quickly with no ill effect. If you are fair skinned, chances are you are liable to get an unpleasant burn unless you are careful. There are three degrees of sunburn, first, second and third, as in most types of burns by acid, fire or heat.

First degree burns result in redness of the skin which soon passes away.

Second degree burns show some destruction of the upper layers of the skin and an effusion of fluid which causes blisters; the blisters eventually break and dry up and the dead scales of the skin peel.

In third degree burns the ultraviolet waves exert an action on the living cells of the skin, bringing about a molecular change which afterwards results in coagulation and death of these cells. The dead cells then are thrown off or are absorbed into the blood. This absorption of detritus excites the nerve ends of the skin, causing extreme pain, blistering and redness. Eventually, because the sweat glands are stopped up, the skin's excretory function is thrown back on the kidneys. The liver also suffers an overload because it must purify the blood of some of the detritus from the dead skin. The body temperature is raised because the skin loses its regulatory powers. Headache, fever, nausea, arrive in greater or lesser degree according to the area of skin affected. The secondary symptoms, the sickness and general low feeling are the results of the toxic condition set up by the burn. If enough of the skin has been burned, and if the victim is not constitutionally strong, death can result from toxemia, which is the cause of most deaths by burns.

SUNSTROKE

The symptoms are headache, dizziness, irritability, seeing things in red or purplish hue; the skin is dry and intensely hot; pupils are contracted; pulse is full and strong, respiration snoring. There may be convulsions; the temperature of the body may go as high as 105° F. or over. The patient should be kept in the shade, and cold water or ice kept against the body to bring down the fever. Have patient drink cold water to which a pinch of salt has been added.

SWAMP GROWING SUMAC

This type of sumac grows in the regions from New England to Minnesota and from Georgia to Texas. This poisonous shrub has white berries and beautiful foliage, but can always be recognized by its fruit, which hangs in drooping clusters. (*Fig. 197.*)

Fig. 197   Swamp Sumac

REMEDIES FOR POISON IVY

One of the most successful remedies for oak, ivy and sumac poisoning is 5 per cent solution of potassium permanganate in water. The solution is applied to affected portions of the skin with a bit of absorbent cotton. The potassium salt destroys the poison, and its only effect on the skin is to leave a brown stain that can be removed easily with 1 per cent solution of oxalic acid or sodium bisulphite.

POISON IVY AND POISON OAK

Poison ivy is a three-leaved American shrub with shining waxlike leaves. It is poisonous to touch, affecting some persons more severely than others. It has dark green leaves with small greenish flowers and white berries. Scientists at the U.S. Public Health Service have recommended a special vanishing cream application to prevent ivy poisoning to a certain extent. Crystals of 10 per cent sodium perborate or of 2 per cent potassium periodate are ground into a fine powder and added to the van-

Fig. 198   *Left,* Poison Ivy; *right,* Poison Oak

ishing cream. This mixture is thoroughly rubbed into the face, arms and hands, before exposure to poison ivy. *Caution—* keep it away from your eyes. As the cream dries the hands and arms are covered with powder. Wash off the powder and put on a new application every four hours if being continuously exposed. To get rid of poison ivy plants dissolve a pound of ammonium sulfamate powder in 1 gallon of water and spray them. Burn the dead leaves but do not come in contact with the smoke as this is as deadly as the live poison ivy.

Poison oak is practically the same as poison ivy in its effect on a person. *(Fig. 198.)* It is good advice to consult a physician in severe cases of either ivy or oak poisoning.

TICKS

Ticks are eight-legged parasites which attack animals and birds as well as human beings, and are the cause of spotted fever. The head, chest and abdomen are all in one; the insect is oval in shape with a flat back of a leathery brownish covering. Although found in plants when young, the large ticks attach themselves by their mouths to the soft flesh of their victim and live on the blood of their victims, growing large, round and red.

Fig. 199   Tick

Rocky Mountain spotted fever is attributed to the infection caused by the hard-shelled tick of the variety technically known as *Dermacentor Andersoni*. Many cases each year are due to tick bites or to crushing infected ticks on the skin, as the disease is never transmitted from person to person. The Rocky Mountain Public Health Service at Bitterroot Range has this to say: "The victim begins with chills, aching head, painful joints and muscles, then a raging fever develops, with a red rash on chest, back, arms and legs." All spotted fever cases occur in April, May and June. Never crush a tick in your finger or smash one against your body. Pull off gently with a pair of tweezers if possible, put in a glass container and burn with gasoline. There is no oil or ointment that can be rubbed on the body that will prevent ticks from attaching themselves. *(Fig. 199.)*

INDEX